IT'S ALL RELATIVE
Key Ideas and Common Misconceptions About Ratio and Prop
Anne Collins and Linda Dacey

Stenhouse Publishers
www.stenhouse.com

Library of Congress Cataloging-in-Publication Data
Collins, Anne, 1956– author.
  It's all relative : key ideas and common misconceptions about ratio and proportion, grades 6–7 / Anne Collins and Linda Dacey.
      p. cm.
  ISBN 978-1-57110-982-8 (pbk. : alk. paper)—ISBN 978-1-62531-009-5 (ebook)
  1. Ratio and proportion—Study and teaching (Middle school)
I. Dacey, Linda, 1962– author. II. Title.
  QA117.C635 2014
  513.2'4—dc23
                                        2013040998

Cover, interior design, and typesetting by MPS Limited

Manufactured in the United States of America
20 19 18 17 16 15 14   9 8 7 6 5 4 3 2 1

Stenhouse Publishers
Portland, Maine

Understanding ratios and proportional relationships and acquiring the accompanying skills associated with their conceptual development are essential. These ideas permeate our daily lives and underpin further study in mathematics and science (Common Core Standards Writing Team 2011). The Common Core State Standards for Mathematics (CCSS-M) identify this area of study as critical at both grades six and seven (NGA and CCSSO 2010).

The thirty modules in this flipchart are designed to engage all students in mathematical learning that develops conceptual understanding, addresses common misconceptions, and builds key ideas essential to future learning. The modules are research based and can be used to support response to intervention (RTI) as well as offer enrichment activities and challenges for all students. The modules are organized in three sections: Representing Ratios; Unit and Scale Factors; and Percents. While building on students' understanding of multiplication and division, the activities in this flipchart will focus on these key ideas:

- Understanding the language of ratios
- Understanding the multiplicative relationships of ratios
- Using tables, tape diagrams, double number line diagrams, and graphs to represent ratios
- Using unit rates and scale factors to solve problems
- Solving multistep ratio and percent problems

The modules increase in complexity by section, though we do not assume that you will focus on only one section at a time nor that you will necessarily complete each component of an activity or section. You can return to many of these activities as students build their mathematical expertise. Each activity begins with the identification of its **Mathematical Focus**, through identification of specific CCSS-M standards. (Either complete standards or portions thereof are provided.) The **Potential Challenges and Misconceptions** associated with those ideas follow. **In the Classroom** then suggests instructional strategies and specific activities to implement with

your students. **Meeting Individual Needs** offers ideas for adjusting the activities to reach a broader range of learners. Opportunities to assess student thinking are often embedded within one section or another. Each activity is supported by one or more reproducibles (located in the appendix), and **References/Further Reading** provides resources for enriching your knowledge of the topic and gathering more ideas.

We encourage you to keep this chart on your desk or next to your plan book so that you will have these ideas at your fingertips throughout the year.

REFERENCES/FURTHER READING

Collins, Anne, and Linda Dacey. 2010. *Zeroing in on Number and Operations: Key Ideas and Common Misconceptions, Grades 7–8.* Portland, ME: Stenhouse.

Common Core Standards Writing Team. 2011. *Progressions for the Common Core State Standards in Mathematics: 6–7, Ratios and Proportional Relationships.* Draft. http://commoncoretools.files.wordpress.com /2012/02/ccss_progression_rp_67_2011_11_12_corrected.pdf.

National Governors Association (NGA) and Council of Chief State School Officers (CCSSO). 2010. *Reaching Higher: The Common Core State Standards Validation Committee—A Report from the National Governors Association Center for Best Practices and the Council of Chief State School Officers.* Washington, DC: NGA Center and CCSSO.

REPRESENTING RATIOS

Squatters

A1

Mathematical Focus

- (6.RP.1) Understand the concept of a ratio; describe a ratio relationship between two quantities.

Potential Challenges and Misconceptions

"Ratios arise in situations in which two (or more) quantities are related" (Common Core Standards Writing Team 2011, 2). The greatest challenge for many students is to think multiplicatively, which requires that students think about relationships among numbers of equal groups, rather than countable objects, and pay attention to two quantities at the same time. Teachers must explicitly model an emphasis on the multiplicative nature of ratios. Many students benefit from acting out or modeling ratios using multiple representations.

In the Classroom

It is exciting for students to act out a situation such as doing squats, jumping rope, or bouncing a ball as many times as possible in a specified period of time as they explore ratios. Divide your class into groups of four and tell them to record the number of squats (or other activity) each student in the group can complete in thirty seconds. After everyone has had a turn, have them repeat the exploration for another activity, such as hopping. Students in each group can take turns acting as the squatter (hopper), the record keeper, the counter, and the timer. Students can use the *What's My Ratio? Recording Sheet* reproducible on page A1 of the appendix to record their data.

Invite student volunteers to share their ratios. If students do not use labels, omit them as you record what they say, and then ask, "Is this ratio about squats or jumping jacks? How do you know?" Then encourage students to use labels as they report. Once you have recorded several examples, facilitate a discussion about the ratios. For example, you might ask, *What does this ratio tell us about the number of squats completed in thirty seconds? Who can state this relationship starting with the phrase "For every . . ."?* or *What can you tell me about this ratio using the word* per? Next ask students to predict, at this rate, how many squats they would complete in one minute.

Meeting Individual Needs

Some students may have physical limitations that prevent them from squatting or hopping. Choose an activity in which all students can participate or provide options such as snapping fingers, typing a name, counting by twelve, drawing stars, or repeating a tongue twister.

REFERENCE/FURTHER READING

Common Core Standards Writing Team. 2011. *Progressions for the Common Core State Standards in Mathematics: 6–7, Ratios and Proportional Relationships*. Draft. http://commoncoretools.files.wordpress.com /2012/02/ccss_progression_rp_67_2011_11_12_corrected.pdf.

Ratio Drama

Mathematical Focus

- (6.RP.1) Understand the concept of a ratio; describe a ratio relationship between two quantities.

Potential Challenges and Misconceptions

Although most students recognize a ratio when it is stated numerically, they often lack recognition of ratio relationships in their daily lives.

In the Classroom

Begin by reading the script provided in the *Script* reproducible on page A2 of the appendix, inviting a student to read one of the roles. After students listen to the script, ask them, "What was different about the ways in which the two people talked? What ratio do you think might represent the number of words Chris said as compared to the number of words Jamie used?" After students estimate, tell them that Chris said 250 words and Jamie said 10. Ask, "So what ratio tells how many words Chris said for every one word Jamie said? How does this ratio compare with your estimate?" In one classroom a student said, "I thought Chris said about one hundred times as many words as Jamie, but it was really only twenty-five." The teacher was able to emphasize the *times as many as* language to highlight the multiplicative relationship. She also asked, "How could we state this relationship using the words *for every*? What about *per*?"

Challenge students to list other aspects of a conversation someone might count, for instance, the number of times someone said "um" compared to the number of words the person spoke. Assign students to groups of four and have them brainstorm their own scenarios. Note that the scenarios may, but do not need to, be related to conversations; however, they should include people in a real-world situation. For example, students might consider the number of ice-cream cones sold in December compared to the number sold in July.

Have students use the *Planning Your Script* reproducible on page A3 of the appendix to help them plan the dramatizations of their scenarios. They will not write scripts, but instead they'll make plans that will allow them to create dramatic examples of ratios. When the groups are ready, have each group present its dramatization while the rest of the students identify the relationship dramatized and estimate the ratio that states the comparison.

Meeting Individual Needs

Presenting a video, rather than reading a script, provides students with visual as well as audio input of an "unbalanced" conversation. Students can view the three-minute animation "Bad Date," one of the "math snacks" found at http://www.mathsnacks.com/.

REFERENCE/FURTHER READING

Van de Walle, John A., Karen Karp, and Jennifer M. Bay-Williams. 2013. *Elementary and Middle School Mathematics: Teaching Developmentally.* 8th ed. New York: Pearson Education.

A2–A3

Mathematical Focus

- (6.RP.3a) Make tables of equivalent ratios; use tables to compare ratios.

Potential Challenges and Misconceptions

There are multiple representations available for determining when ratios are equivalent. However, when using tables or lists, many students think additively and add the same number to both quantities in a ratio to create an equivalent ratio. It is extremely important for students to understand and use the multiplicative relationship.

In the Classroom

Begin this lesson with an assessment question to inform your sense of which students might need more support during this work: *Tell me what you think the term* equivalent *means in mathematics.* Record your students' responses on the class conjecture board. Tell them they are going to investigate equivalent ratios. Then pose the following problem while projecting, or copying on the board, the ratio table shown below.

Jamal is having pizzas at his birthday party. He knows that he needs 2 pizzas to feed 6 people. How many pizzas should he order to feed 24 people?

Challenge students to complete the following ratio table, illustrating equivalent ratios that might be used to determine the number of pizzas Jamal needs.

Pizzas	2	4	10		
People	6			16	24

As the students work, walk around and observe if any students are using addition to complete the table. For example, some students may suggest 8 pizzas for 4 people, as 4 is two more than 2, and 8 is two more than 6. Ask, "How many people can you feed for every 2 pizzas? Can you show me what that means for the 4 pizzas?"

When appropriate, ask student volunteers to share their solutions. Ask questions to stress the importance of using the multiplicative identity. For example: *What was the 2 multiplied by to get a product of 6? How could you use that factor to find the number of people those 12 pizzas can feed?* Then ask why multiplying by the same factor results in equivalent fractions. If no one refers to the multiplicative identity (one), introduce the language to the conversation and make sure students recognize how they multiplied by one. Finally, have students reflect back on their discussion of the meaning of *equivalent* to see if there is anything they want to add, revise, or delete from the conjecture list. Then assign the problem set in the *Equivalent Ratios* reproducible on page A4 of the appendix.

Meeting Individual Needs

Students may model the pizzas-to-people ratio using differently colored tiles. As they model the multiplication through duplication, encourage them to use the language of two pizzas *for every* six people.

REFERENCE/FURTHER READING

Lobato, Joanne, Amy B. Ellis, Randall I. Charles, and Rose Mary Zbiek. 2010. *Developing Essential Understanding of Ratios, Proportions, and Proportional Reasoning for Teaching Mathematics: Grades 6–8.* Reston, VA: National Council of Teachers of Mathematics.

Mathematical Focus

- (6.RP.3) Use ratio reasoning to solve real-world and mathematical problems, e.g., by reasoning about tape diagrams.

Potential Challenges and Misconceptions

Many students have used tables to represent ratios, but few have worked with tape (or bar) diagrams to show ratio relationships. Often students are unsure about what data to use or how to use given data when solving word problems. The use of tape diagrams is an effective strategy for visualizing the data given in real-world situations as well as for determining an unknown quantity. Tape diagrams effectively model the relationship among the parts being compared to the whole. The whole is divided into equivalent cells, which are labeled to illustrate the various parts. So when comparing boys to girls, for example, some of the cells would be labeled "girls," the remaining "boys," and the total diagram would represent total students. Tape diagrams clearly identify the ratio of those parts so if the ratio of 5 girls to 7 boys is being explored, 5 cells would be labeled "girls," 7 labeled "boys," and the 12 cells would represent the total number of students.

In the Classroom

Present this problem:

> Dane and Quinn collect sports cards. Dane has 4 cards for every 3 cards that Quinn has. If Dane gives Quinn $\frac{1}{2}$ of his cards, what will be the new ratio of Dane's cards to Quinn's?

Draw and explain a tape diagram of the "before" ratio before challenging students to model the "after" ratio to solve the problem. This before-and-after model (shown in the figure below) allows students to visualize the changes that occur in the problem. Notice the new ratio is 2:5. Ask if this means that Dane has two cards and Quinn has five cards.

Before assigning the problems in the *How Might Ratios Look?* reproducible on page A5, invite the students to model and solve the following problem:

> Mia and Nora each have a collection of mystery books. For every 3 mystery books Mia has, Nora has 5. Mia decides to give half of her books to Nora. What will be the new ratio of Mia's mystery books to Nora's?

In this situation, students should be able to represent the problem as shown in the following figure. To determine the ratio, however, all parts need to be the same, which requires that the model be partitioned.

The new ratio is 3:11. Ask if Mia has three books and Nora eleven books.

Meeting Individual Needs

Some students may need more explicit directions to understand that each component in the tape diagrams must be the same size and shape. To enable students who need this support, provide them with Cuisenaire rods that they can use to model the situations. After building the models, they should draw sketches of how the models look.

REFERENCE/FURTHER READING

Murata, Aki. 2008. "Mathematics Teaching and Learning as a Mediating Process: The Case of Tape Diagrams." *Mathematical Thinking and Learning* 10 (4): 374–406.

Mathematical Focus

- (6.RP.1) Understand the concept of a ratio; describe a ratio relationship between two quantities.
- (6.RP.3) Reason about double number line diagrams.

Potential Challenges and Misconceptions

Few students have had experience with double number lines and may not recognize that the connections between the lines illustrate that there is a relationship between the two. It is helpful to engage students in exploring double number lines and their multiplicative relationship before expecting students to apply them in problem-solving situations.

In the Classroom

One teacher draws two number lines on her tiled floor with liquid shoe polish. (Custodians find the shoe polish easy to wash off.) Then she asks student volunteers to model the ratio 3 parts chocolate chips to 5 parts almonds. She provides them with sticky notes with the numerals 3, 5, 9, 15, 21, and 35 and masking tape to mark approximate intervals. The students place the sticky notes where they belong on the double number line. The rest of the class observes, noting the students' conversations and decisions. Finally, the students label the number lines as shown in the figure below.

The teacher asks the observing students to comment on how their peers made their decisions and whether or not they agree with those decisions. The teacher then asks all the students to describe what relationship is shown. Sarah states, "The difference is plus 3, then plus 6, then plus 12 on the first line and plus 5, then plus 10, then plus 20 on the bottom."

The teacher asks if anyone noticed anything else. Scott explains, "If you multiply 3 by 3 you get 9, and 3 by 7 you get 21 for the first line, and on the second line if you multiply 5 by 3 you

get 15, and 5 by 7 gives 35. That keeps the ratio of 3 to 5."

This teacher reinforces the multiplicative relationship by saying, "So you think multiplication by the same number is important. What property do we use when we multiply each value on each of the number lines by the same factor?" She asks her students to each make a table to check their thinking. To make sure that students understand the ratios are all equivalent, she asks, "Is the ratio twenty-one to thirty-five greater than, equal to, or less than the ratio three to five?" Once students have confirmed the ratios are equivalent, she assigns the *Double Up* reproducible from page A6 of the appendix.

Meeting Individual Needs

For students who need more scaffolding, it might be helpful to actually mark intervals on the number lines until the students gain more experience with the multiplicative reasoning. It may also be appropriate to make "slide rules" for the students to manipulate as they develop their reasoning. A *Ratio Slide Rules* template can be found on page A7 of the appendix.

REFERENCE/FURTHER READING

Lamon, Susan. 2012. *Teaching Fractions and Ratios for Understanding: Essential Content Knowledge and Instructional Strategies for Teachers.* New York: Routledge.

Comparing Ratios

Mathematical Focus

- (6.RP.3) Use ratio reasoning to solve real-world and mathematical problems.

Potential Challenges and Misconceptions

Too often students apply algorithms or formulas erroneously. Helping students develop the ability to estimate and compare ratios informally before introducing such techniques provides opportunities for students to reason quantitatively while developing conceptual foundations for later work.

In the Classroom

Present the following information to students:

There were 20 problems on the quiz.

Student A answered 4 problems correctly for every 1 problem answered incorrectly.

Student B answered 7 problems correctly for every 3 problems answered incorrectly.

Have the students work individually for about four minutes, writing down everything this information tells them. Circulate with a clipboard as they write, noting those students who have several ideas and those that have fewer. Then have students turn to their partners to exchange ideas. Again circulate, this time paying attention to the words the students use to describe and compare the ratios.

Have pairs share one idea at a time with the whole group for as many times as it is possible to do so without repeating. Record each of the comments for all to see. With each suggestion, ask other students if they agree or disagree and discuss as necessary. Consider asking the following questions if no one brings up these ideas:

- *How many problems on the quiz did Student A solve correctly? How do you know?*
- *Who solved more problems correctly on the quiz, Student A or Student B? How do you know? Does anyone else have another way to find this answer?*

Next display the questions below and encourage students to share their thinking with the class.

Which of the following ratios would you rather have describe how your correct answers compared to your incorrect answers?

5:6 or 6:5
10:3 or 30:9
7:3 or 14:6

Assign the *Which Ratio Do You Want?* reproducible on page A8 in the appendix for more practice.

Meeting Individual Needs

Encourage some students to create tables, tape diagrams, or double number lines of equivalent ratios to help them compare ratios.

REFERENCE/FURTHER READING

Sharp, Janet M., and Barbara Adams. 2003. "Using a Pattern Table to Solve Contextualized Proportion Problems." *Mathematics Teaching in the Middle School* 8 (8): 432–39.

Mathematical Focus

- (6.RP.3a) Plot the pairs of values on the coordinate plane. Use tables to compare ratios.
- (7.RP.2a) Test for equivalent ratios on a coordinate plane.

Potential Challenges and Misconceptions

A ratio is, by definition, a comparison between two quantities, and a ratio can be represented on a Cartesian coordinate plane. Most students do not realize this. They do not have experience with finding a ratio from a graph. Further, they think of coordinate pairs only as points on a grid, not as relationships between two quantities. It is important that students recognize this relationship as it sets the foundational understanding for thinking about ratio as slope.

In the Classroom

Project the graph *Which Is Saltier?* from page A9 of the appendix. Challenge your students to work in small groups to interpret the graph and talk about what they notice about the rays. Give the students chart paper and ask them to list any similarities or differences in the rays. When they've completed that task, direct the students to hang their papers around the room and conduct a gallery walk. Instruct each group to post one positive comment and one question on each paper. In one classroom the lists included these observations:

> The steeper the graph the more water there is in the mixture.
> We can take the points and put them in a table.
> One ray has more water for the same amount of salt.

Discuss their observations. Begin by focusing on particular points, for example when there are 4 units of salt, and ask students what they can conclude. If the students do not identify which of the rays represents the saltier mixture, ask them which they think would taste saltier. Be sure they understand why the ray that is closest to the salt axis represents the saltier mixture. To ensure your students understand this concept, challenge them to graph the salt to water ratios for 2:3 and 3:4 on the same set of axes. Tell them to list all the observations they can make about the two graphs. Ask for volunteers to share their ideas. Look for responses like these:

> Both graphs have a lattice point at $x = 12$.
> They both have a lattice point at $y = 6$.
> The graph of 3:4 is steeper than the graph of 2:3.
> The graph of 2:3 represents the saltier mixture.

Pair your students and have them play the *Match It* game from the appendix (pages A10–A14). Students shuffle the cards and deal them faceup in an array. The object of the game is to match each graph with its table. The first player selects a card and tries to match it to its corresponding representation. That student must convince his or her opponent that the cards are equivalent. If they *are* equivalent, the student keeps the two cards and the next player takes a turn. If the cards are *not* equivalent, they are returned to the array and the next player takes a turn. If there is a disagreement, the teacher may play the role of referee and tell the students whether they are correct. Play alternates between the two students until all the cards are matched. The student with the most cards wins the game. After students play the game, assign the *Graph It* reproducible, found on pages A15–A16 in the appendix.

Meeting Individual Needs

Some students will benefit from making a table of the data shown in the graph representing the amount of salt in two solutions of water. When discussing the idea of the steepness of a ray, it is important for many students to explicitly use language referring to the axes, such as *The ray that approaches the axis labeled "Salt" is saltier*, instead of just referring to the steepness of the ray.

To offer some students a challenge, have them play a different version of the *Match It* game. Students should arrange the cards facedown and play like Concentration. If a student turns over two matching cards, he or she keeps them; otherwise, the student turns them facedown again and play continues.

REFERENCE/FURTHER READING

Ercole, Leslie K., Marny Frantz, and George Ashline. 2011. "Multiple Ways to Solve Proportions." *Mathematics Teaching in the Middle School* 16 (8): 483–90.

Mathematical Focus

- (6.RP.3) Use ratio reasoning to solve real-world and mathematical problems.
- (7.RP.2a) Test for equivalent ratios.

Potential Challenges and Misconceptions

Too often students are shown a procedure for converting ratios to decimals without using any quantitative reasoning. This lack of understanding is compounded when students use calculators to make conversions before they understand in which order they should enter the values. When asked if a conversion makes sense, students often reply, "Well, that is what the calculator got." Students need multiple opportunities to learn how to determine the reasonableness of their answers.

In the Classroom

One teacher believes strongly that students who are adept at working with ratios in fraction and decimal forms have an easier time building on this knowledge when performing problem-solving tasks. She instructs her students to work in small groups to complete the *Conversion Tables* sheet on page A17 and to record any and all patterns they notice. As they work, she asks questions such as *Is there an answer in the table that you know? How can you use that information to find another decimal?* After an allotted period of time, she invites student volunteers to share their reasoning for the first table. While a few students know that they can change a ratio to a decimal using division, others suggest alternative strategies. As this thinking supports students' sense making, the teacher wants to emphasize it.

Manny: Our group started with the commonest ones, like $\frac{1}{2}$ and $\frac{1}{4}$. Like, 4:8 is $\frac{1}{2}$, which is 0.50, so we filled that in the chart. We also knew that 2:8 is the same as 1:4, which is a quarter, so we put in 0.25.

Sam: We also figured 2:8 was the same as 1:4, which we know is a quarter, or 0.25 . . . it's like 25 cents. Then we added the 0.25 to the 0.50 and got 0.75. So, like we said, 1:4 plus 2:4 must be 3:4 and be 0.75, like 75 cents. Since 3:4 is the same as 6:8, we wrote that on the chart. We figured that 3:8 is halfway between 2:8 and 4:8, so we divided 0.25 by 2 and got 0.125. So

then we knew we could just keep adding that to finish the table.

Lucas: We know you can change a ratio to a decimal by dividing. So, we divided each numerator by each denominator. We got the same answers as Manny and Sam.

The class discusses each strategy the students have shared. At the end of the lesson this teacher assigns an exit card and asks her students to find an equivalent decimal for 3:8.

Meeting Individual Needs

Students who struggle with division can use calculators to do the conversions if needed. However, it is often necessary to work with those students to help them understand the order in which to enter the numbers and how to determine if their answers are reasonable.

REFERENCE/FURTHER READING

Lappan, Glenda, James Fey, William Fitzgerald, Susan Friel, and Elisabeth Phillips. 2012. *Comparing and Scaling: Ratio, Proportion, and Percent.* Upper Saddle River, NJ: Pearson Prentice Hall.

A Round and a Round the PIe

Mathematical Focus

- (6.RP.1) Understand the concept of a ratio; describe a ratio relationship between two quantities.
- (6.RP.3a) Make tables of equivalent ratios and plot the pairs of values on the coordinate plane.

Potential Challenges and Misconceptions

Many students do not realize that pi is the ratio between the circumference of a circle and its radius. Too often teachers leave the ratio relationship in circles unexplored, placing emphasis solely on formulas. Many students who experience this approach are unable to determine the reasonableness of their answers since they have no sense of the value of pi.

In the Classroom

One teacher engages his students in modeling the ratio of the circumference of a circle to its radius. He brings students to an open space and draws a large circle on the floor with liquid shoe polish. He asks for two volunteers, one to be a dowel or rope holder and one to be a walker. He places a dowel or piece of rope on the floor between the center point and a point marked on the circumference of the circle. He instructs the walker to walk heel to toe from the marked point to the center, counting the number of steps. Next, he asks the same walker to count the number of steps while walking heel to toe along the circumference. He records these numbers and asks students to describe any relationships they see.

Students then investigate the same relationship with different-size circles. He groups the students into triads; each group has a recorder, a dowel-and-rope holder, and a walker. He provides each dowel holder with a meter-long dowel or a meter stick and four pieces of clothesline cut to various lengths. The dowel holder attaches the end of one of the ropes to one end of the dowel with a staple, places that end of the dowel on the ground, and holds the other end of the dowel vertically. The walker holds the other end of the rope, keeping the rope taut, and uses that as a compass with which to draw a circle on the floor using colored chalk. The recorder makes a table on which to record the length of the rope (the radius) and the circumference of the circle it creates; see the *Pi Recording Sheet* on page A18 for a template. The group repeats the process with all four lengths of clothesline. The teacher challenges the groups to explore what happens to the information about the circles as the length of the rope changes.

Students record their data on a large class recording sheet as well as in their notebooks. He then leads the class in a discussion.

In one class, a student said, "I thought it would be three times because that is like the value of pi."

One student noted, "That's what I thought too, but it didn't work with my data."

Another student commented, "I notice that it takes about six lengths of rope to complete the circle." Still another student erroneously commented, "I think I know the formula; is it $C = \pi r$?"

In this particular classroom, the teacher challenges the students to test their conjectures and to revise as necessary. He gave these students time to work and then one commented, "Wait, the ratios are about 1:6, and our radius was 3, so we double the radius to get the formula $C = 2\pi r$."

After allotting time for further exploration and discussion, assign the *Missing Data* reproducible on page A19.

Meeting Individual Needs

The order in which you invite students to share their work is important. It is helpful to call on students who are less confident of their measures after other students have had a chance to share their results, whether correct or not, in order to provide a risk-free environment. You could extend this activity by instructing students to graph the circumference in relation to the radius.

REFERENCE/FURTHER READING

Touval, Ayana. 2009. "Walking a Radian." *Mathematics Teacher* 102 (9): 692–96.

Mathematical Focus

- (6.RP.3) Use ratio reasoning to solve real-world and mathematical problems.

Potential Challenges and Misconceptions

Solving word problems has historically caused teachers and students angst. Working through ratio problems has been particularly difficult for many students since ratios do not always represent the actual number of items being compared. Effective problem solving involves identifying and using an appropriate strategy, creating an appropriate representation to support one's reasoning, and justifying that reasoning and the reasonableness of the answer, all of which pose a great challenge to many students. All of these components are articulated in the Common Core State Standards for Mathematical Practice.

In the Classroom

One teacher asks her students to model this problem in any way that makes sense to them:

> Ming and Omar have markers in the ratio of 5 to 8. If Omar gives one-half of his markers to Ming, what is the new ratio of markers?

Then she asks volunteers to explain their strategies to the class. Lukas shares his before-and-after tape diagrams (see figure below).

Before

Ming [| | | |]

Omar [| | | | | | |]

After

Ming [| | | | | ┆┆┆┆]

Omar [| | |]

Claire shows her before-and-after table (see figure below).

	Ming	Omar
Before	5	8
After	9	4

Stephie shares her graph (see following figure).

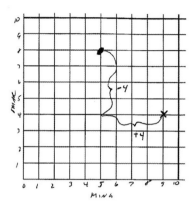

This teacher then asks her students how the representations are the same and different. Students recognize that they all show the before data and the after data. Some students think that the tape diagram makes it easier to see the ratio. One student points out, "The table might be easier to make, especially if the numbers are large." After the discussion, the teacher assigns the ratio problems 1–3 from the *Choose Your Own Method* reproducible on page A20 in the appendix. She reserves question 4 for students who need a challenge.

Meeting Individual Needs

Some students may need help in determining an appropriate model to use. Often these students do best when they model the problem using concrete materials, followed by a pictorial representation. It also helps some students to show both the before and the after representations, even after other students have moved beyond that need.

REFERENCE/FURTHER READING
70 Must-Know Word Problems series. 2009. Columbus, OH: Frank Schaffer.

A21–A22

Mathematical Focus

- (6.RP.2) Understand the concept of a unit rate a/b associated with a ratio $a:b$ with $b \neq 0$, and use rate language in the context of a ratio relationship.
- (6.RP.3) Use ratio and rate reasoning to solve real-world and mathematical problems.
- (7.RP.1) Compute unit rates associated with ratios of fractions, including ratios of lengths, areas and other quantities measured in like or different units.

Potential Challenges and Misconceptions

When given the ratio of $6 for three cards, students usually recognize that the unit rate is $2 per card. When the ratio does not involve such simple numbers or when one number is not divisible by the other, such recognition is far less likely. For example, if José can read twenty pages in thirty minutes, then twenty pages per thirty minutes can be considered his rate of reading. Students should also recognize that this is the same as two pages per three minutes and as two-thirds page per minute. The latter form is the rate expressed as a unit rate, which can be used to find missing values or to compare values.

In the Classroom

One teacher begins by assigning the following problem, which she projects for the class to see.

> Natasha earned $42.50 for baby-sitting for 5 hours last night. At this rate, how much will she be paid to baby-sit for 7.5 hours?

She instructs each small group to complete its work and be ready to share its thinking later with the class.

Caden's group makes a table (see figure below) and then reports that it was easy because the students had to work only with wholes and halves.

Hours	Pay
5	$42.50
2.5	$21.25
7.5	$63.75

Manny explains that his group wanted to find out how much money Natasha made each hour and found that $42.50 \div 5 = \$8.50$. They then multiplied the hourly rate by 7.5 to find the total. He ends his report by saying, "We can use this number to find what she made whatever the hours were."

The teacher explains that Manny's group found the unit rate because it was the amount Natasha was paid for one hour. She then asks, "How can we find the unit rate in the table that Caden's group made?" The students agree that for each row, the quotient is $8.50. Then the teacher asks each student to talk with a partner to decide which of these methods each of them would use to find out how much Natasha would be paid for nine hours. The students think it would be easiest to use the unit rate and multiply. They also decide that depending on the number of hours, for example, fifteen, a table could be the easiest way to organize the information. This teacher then assigns the *Ratios and Unit Rates* reproducible on pages A21–A22 in the appendix.

Meeting Individual Needs

Students must recognize that *per hour* or */hr.* is a shorthand version of *per 1 hour*. You may want to use *per 1 hour* for some students. Have students write phrases associated with unit rates in their journals, and add the following to a word wall or anchor chart: *It takes 2.5 hours to mow 1 lawn. The unit rate is 2.5 hours per lawn, 2.5 hr./1 lawn, or 2.5 hr./lawn.*

REFERENCE/FURTHER READING

National Council of Teachers of Mathematics. 2009. "Palette of Problems/Menu of Problems—Palette of Problems." *Mathematics Teaching in the Middle School* 15 (3): 132–33.

Different Unit Rates

Mathematical Focus

- (6.RP.2) Understand the concept of a unit rate a/b associated with a ratio $a:b$ with $b \neq 0$, and use rate language in the context of a ratio relationship.
- (6.RP.3) Use ratio and rate reasoning to solve real-world and mathematical problems.
- (7.RP.1) Compute unit rates associated with ratios of fractions.

Potential Challenges and Misconceptions

Some students ignore the importance of the order in a given ratio or rate. A ratio of two quantities can be expressed from two perspectives, depending on which quantity is being compared to the other; for example, a ratio could be expressed as 8 cups of rolled oats:2 batches of oatmeal cookies or as 2 batches of oatmeal cookies:8 cups of rolled oats. You might care most about the portion of a batch of cookies you could make with 1 cup of rolled oats or about how many cups of rolled oats it would take to make 1 batch of cookies. The same is true of unit rates. Students need to be able to recognize which unit rate is most useful in a given situation. Deciding which rate is best suited to the situation reinforces the language of rate within a ratio relationship and requires students to focus on the order of the given ratio.

In the Classroom

To review the usefulness of unit rates, display the following table and ask students to find the missing value.

Gasoline

Total Cost	Number of Gallons
$3.69	1
$7.38	2
$11.07	3
$14.76	4
	7

As students work, note those that use additive techniques (that is, they add $3.69 to $14.76 three times to find the cost of three more gallons) and those who use the unit rate and multiply by seven to find the missing value. Have students discuss each method. For this situation, students might find either method appropriate. Ask them which method they would use to find the cost of one hundred gallons at this rate. Summarize that multiplying by the unit rate can be particularly helpful and efficient when large numbers are involved.

Next ask, "How might I find the cost of 1 gallon if all I know is that the ratio of total cost to gallons is $11.07:3 gallons?" Once students identify that you would use division, have them use their calculators to confirm that the quotient for each row (cost/gallons) is the same. Reinforce students' understanding of ratios and rate by saying, "When we stop to buy gas, we pay the same amount for each gallon we buy, so the unit rate is the same. When the unit rate is the same, the ratios are equivalent, and the relationship between total cost and number of gallons is proportional. If, however, there was a gas station special, like buy thirteen gallons and get two gallons free, the total cost and number of gallons would not be proportional."

Finally, pose these questions about the data in the table for students to consider with their partners:

> If I have only $20, how many gallons of gas can I buy?
> What if I have only $1? How many gallons can I buy?
> What is the unit rate for a gallon of gas?

Have students discuss their thinking as a large group. Emphasize that two related quantities can be compared in two different ways. That is, there are two ratios we can write to describe their relationship, with two associated unit rates. Assign the *Cooking* reproducible on page A23 for additional practice.

Meeting Individual Needs

For students who are not yet strong in their understanding or use of unit rates, focus on just $a:b$ or $b:a$ but not both potential relationships, unless you provide both related tables or ratios.

REFERENCE/FURTHER READING

Carbone, Katie. 2008. "Measuring Up: Lesson 3: What's Your Rate?" Illuminations. http://illuminations.nctm.org/LessonDetail.aspx?ID=L511.

Mathematical Focus

- (6.RP.3) Use ratio and rate reasoning to solve real-world and mathematical problems.
- (7.RP.2b) Identify the constant of proportionality (unit rate) in tables, graphs, equations, diagrams, and verbal descriptions of proportional relationships.

Potential Challenges and Misconceptions

The ability to determine and compare unit pricing is a critical consumer skill, yet so often consumers are confused by such information, particularly when measurement units are involved. Often people assume that the larger a container of food is, the better the price. Yet if they checked the unit rate for different-sized containers, they could make a more informed decision and recognize that it may be less expensive to buy two smaller containers of a particular product rather than one larger container. Multiple representations can help students better understand the proportional thinking associated with unit rates. Students may also overgeneralize rules they have learned about rounding. Make sure students understand that in a store, money is always rounded up to the nearest cent.

In the Classroom

Begin by asking students how much they would pay for one pencil if they bought pencils at a sale price of two for $0.99. Make sure students agree that one pencil would cost $0.50, as stores round up prices to the closet whole cent. Then present the following problem to students:

> Apple Snacks are on sale today. You can buy 4 Apple Snacks for $5. Choose four other numbers of Apple Snacks you might buy. What would be their total cost?

Divide the class into three groups. Have the students in one group represent this information in tables, students in the second group use tape diagrams, and students in the third group use graphs. The students in each group can work alone or in pairs. Ask one student or pair from each group to present its work to the class. Ask questions like: *Where is the one piece of information you were given? How did you use this information to include other equivalent ratios? Which ratio shows the unit price?* (Or, if the unit price is not included in the students' work, *How could you use this information to find the unit price?*) *Are all of the ratios shown equivalent? How do you know?*

To emphasize to students that when all of the ratios are equivalent, the relationship is proportional, add a counterexample, such as twelve Apple Snacks for sixteen dollars, and ask whether it fits their data.

Present students the following problems, or use real local grocery flyers and create your own, similar questions:

3 cans of corn for $3.50	Turkeys: 12 lb. for $8.99	Bananas: $0.69 per lb.
What does 1 can cost?	What does 1 lb. cost?	What do $7\frac{1}{2}$ lb. cost?

Circulate as student pairs are working, posing questions such as *Can you find another way to solve that? Can you convince me? How does the turkey problem relate to the banana question? How do you know your solution is correct? Why are you rounding up?*

After an allotted period of time, invite student volunteers to share the strategies and representations they used, their solutions, and how the three problems are similar and dissimilar. When discussing the solutions to the problems, be sure that the students understand that the first two problems are asking the same thing—to find the unit rate—and that the third question *gives the unit rate* and asks students to use that to find the *total cost*.

Provoke a conversation that prods students to articulate why they need to divide for the first two problems but have to multiply for the third. Ask how the division and multiplication connect to their representations. Ask them how they might convince someone who disagrees with their solutions or choice of operations. Finally, make sure students understand that unit rates can be used to compare ratios. After this discussion, assign the *Camping Out* reproducible on page A24 of the appendix.

Meeting Individual Needs

For students who are uncertain about how to use each of the representations (table, tape diagram, and graph) for these problems, provide them with a copy of the sample solutions in the *Possible Representations* reproducible on page A25. The reproducible illustrates solutions for the three grocery-ad problems presented earlier. Tell the students to use those samples as a reference sheet as they work toward becoming more proficient with these models.

REFERENCE/FURTHER READING

Telese, James A., and Jesse Abete Jr. 2002. "Diet, Ratios, Proportions: A Healthy Mix." *Mathematics Teaching in the Middle School* 8 (1): 8–13.

Area and Unit Rates

Mathematical Focus

- (6.RP.3d) Use ratio reasoning to convert measurement units.
- (7.RP.1) Compute unit rates associated with ratios of fractions, including ratios of lengths, areas and other quantities measured in like or different units.
- (7.RP.2c) Represent proportional relationships by equations.

Potential Challenges and Misconceptions

Students and adults often have misconceptions about area, thinking, for example, that if the side lengths of a rectangle double, so does its area. This lack of true understanding of the multiplicative relationship of lengths to area causes them to also underestimate, for example, the number of square inches in a square foot. Providing both concrete experiences and pictures on graph paper are necessary to help students develop an accurate sense of these units.

In the Classroom

One teacher engages his students in experimenting with how many inches are in a foot, how many inches are in a yard, and how many feet are in a yard. This teacher divides students into pairs and provides them with chalk, rulers, and yardsticks. Students are instructed to use their chalk and ruler to mark one foot on the blacktop area of the schoolyard or on their tiled floor. On that foot they are told to make a tick mark for every inch. They repeat this using the yardstick, marking each foot in the yard. They are then asked to determine the number of inches in one yard based on their chalk drawings. He asks his students to record their findings as unit rates and equations. He calls on student volunteers to share their thinking, making sure that a variety of unit rates and equations are identified, and records them on an anchor chart, which he posts. He records them under headings of unit rates ("Inches," "Feet," etc.) and "Equations" so that students can refer to them at any time.

Inches	Feet	Yards	Equation
36		1	$\frac{1}{36}$ yd. = 1 in.
	3	1	3 ft. = 1 yd.
	1	$\frac{1}{3}$	$\frac{1}{3}$ yd. = 1 ft.

He asks students to work in pairs to find the following missing values:

There are _____ inches in 5 yards.
There are _____ feet in 150 inches.

There are _____ inches in 6.5 feet.
There is _____ of a yard in 24 inches.

Again he has a few students share their strategies.

Following this work with linear units, the teacher extends their work with unit measures to include square units as in an area model. He instructs his students to measure a square yard and within that square yard to mark or draw as many square feet as possible. Once the students have marked nine square feet, he tells them to subdivide one of the square feet into as many square inches as possible. He asks them to calculate how many square inches are in a square foot (144), followed by how many square inches are in a square yard (1,296). Again, he instructs his students to record as many unit rates and equations as possible. Next, he asks student volunteers to share their observations. Melody's group reports, "We didn't know that if you made square inches you really got squares. We just thought it was something we memorized but now we understand there is a huge difference between an inch and a square inch."

Next, this teacher directs his students to draw a representation—on either the blacktop or the tiled floor—of a square that is 2 yards by 2 yards and to calculate how many square feet there are in this enlarged square. He tells them to focus on what happens to the area of this square compared with the area of a 1-yard-by-1-yard square. He asks them to find the number of square feet in 2,880 square inches. After students present a variety of solutions, he assigns the problems from the *Covering Spaces* reproducible on page A26.

Meeting Individual Needs

You may wish to assign roles in each pair so that all students can experience success. All students who are able can help to draw the lines in the figures. Other possible roles include counter, unit factor identifier, equation identifier, and recorder. Many students are amazed to discover there are 144 square inches in 1 square foot. Even though they know how to find the area of a rectangle, they tend to think there are 24 square inches in 1 square foot. It can be helpful to have students first sketch how large they think a square foot would be before they make actual models.

REFERENCE/FURTHER READING

Lobato, Joanne, Amy B. Ellis, Randall I. Charles, and Rose Mary Zbiek. 2010. *Developing Essential Understanding of Ratios, Proportions, and Proportional Reasoning for Teaching Mathematics, Grades 6–8*. Reston, VA: National Council of Teachers of Mathematics.

Mathematical Focus

- (6.RP.3) Use ratio and rate reasoning to solve real-world and mathematical problems.
- (7.RP.2b) Identify the constant of proportionality in tables, graphs, equations, diagrams, and verbal descriptions of proportional relationships.

Potential Challenges and Misconceptions

Without a chance to "play" with enlarging and reducing cartoons, pictures, or figures, students are unlikely to internalize the concept that for an image to be proportional, *all* dimensions in the original must be changed by the same value while the angles remain the same. The numerical relationship between the original and the image is known as the *scale factor*. If an original figure is enlarged, the scale factor is greater than one, and if it is reduced, the scale factor is a proper fraction.

In the Classroom

On graph paper, have students draw a square that is 2 inches by 2 inches. Then have them draw a 3-inch-by-3-inch square. Ask what they notice. Most students will state that both figures are squares, but that one is larger. Students might even use the term *similar* in an informal manner. Next, ask them to identify the ratio between the lengths of the sides of the larger square and the sides of the smaller one. Once they identify the ratio as 3:2, ask, "How many times longer is the length of the longer side than the length of the shorter side?" (1.5 times longer). Explain that we call this the *scale factor* and put the term on your word wall. Follow this question by asking, "How many times greater is the area of the larger square compared to the area of the smaller square?" ($3^2:2^2$ or 9:4 or $2\frac{1}{4}$ times greater). Explain that when we enlarge or reduce images, we want to do so proportionally, so that the result has the same shape and its corresponding sides are proportional. Ask, "What would happen to the original square if we scaled the length by a factor of 2 and the width by a factor of 5? Would the original square and the new figure be proportional? How do you know?"

Next have students find the areas and perimeters of the 2-by-2 square and the 3-by-3 square and talk about what they notice. (The perimeters, since they are linear, have the same scale factor as the lengths. But the areas, which are two-dimensional, are the squares of the lengths, creating a ratio of 9:4, for a scale factor of 2.25, as both the width and the length were increased.)

Next give each student two same-size elastics, a copy of the *Scaling Scotties* reproducible on pages A27–A29 in the appendix, and a sheet of plain white paper. Students tape the blank piece of paper next to the reproducible (on the right of the reproducible for students who are right-handed and on the left for those who are left-handed) and loop the two elastics together to make a "stretcher." Make sure students understand the task, particularly that the connection point of the stretcher needs to trace along the outline of the Scottie. Encourage the students to "trace" the Scottie multiple times until they make a Scottie that is the image of the original. After a student completes the enlargement, he or she should respond to the questions in a math journal or notebook. Have students discuss their responses.

To assess their understanding after the discussion, assign these three questions as a "ticket to leave."

- A 5 ft.–by–6 ft. rectangle has been proportionally reduced by a scale factor of $\frac{1}{2}$ What are the new dimensions of the rectangle?
- A 3 in.–by–4 in. rectangle has been proportionally enlarged to a 4.5 in.–by–6 in. rectangle. What is the scale factor?
- A $\frac{1}{2}$ in.–by–$\frac{3}{4}$ in. rectangle has been increased by a scale factor of 2.5. What are the new dimensions of the rectangle?

Meeting Individual Needs

If students have dexterity issues, you may want to assign geometric figures such as a triangle, rhombus, or trapezoid to enlarge, as polygons do not require as much eye-hand coordination as the Scottie. See the *Scaling Houses* reproducible on page A30 in the appendix.

REFERENCE/FURTHER READING

Lappan, Glenda, Elizabeth Phillips, Susan Friel, James Fey, and William Fitzgerald. 2004. *Stretching and Shrinking: Understanding Similarity.* Connected Mathematics 2. Upper Saddle River, NJ: Prentice Hall.

Mathematical Focus

- (6.RP.3) Use ratio and rate reasoning to solve real-world and mathematical problems.
- (7.RP.2b) Identify the constant of proportionality (unit rate) in tables, graphs, equations, diagrams, and verbal descriptions of proportional relationships.

Potential Challenges and Misconceptions

The use of double number lines to represent proportional relationships is a relatively new approach for many students. Many students become confused initially because each number line represents a different unit and may have a different scale. Students need to think about the double number lines as representing ratios rather than consecutive integers, like single number lines do in arithmetic. Most students need a lot of practice before they fully understand that the double number lines are a visual way in which to show two quantities and how they are related to each other.

In the Classroom

Project the following problem and the accompanying double number line (see figure below) on the whiteboard and ask your students to list everything they can about the relationship displayed. Once the list is complete, challenge the students to solve the problem.

> When I printed your homework problems, it took the copy machine 45 seconds to print 60 copies. At this rate, how many copies can be made in 72 seconds?

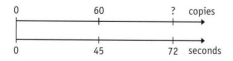

After an allotted period of time, invite student volunteers to share their strategies and solutions. Use a document camera to project student work if possible; otherwise, make transparencies from the reproducible to enable student reporters to illustrate how they thought about the problem. If you have been recently working with scale factors, students will probably note that the seconds have been increased from 45 to 72, which is a scale factor of 1.6. To be proportional, the same scale factor must be applied to the seconds, so they must multiply 60 by 1.6 to find that 72 copies will take 96 seconds.

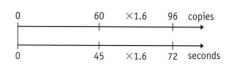

Note that some students may find the unit rate per second by dividing both the 60 and the 45 by 45. Then they would multiply this unit factor of 1.33/sec. by 72 to find the number of copies that can be made in 72 seconds. Some students may even set up a proportion to solve this problem. If so, help them see how that method relates to the double number line. For a deeper understanding, examine the explanation between unit rates, scale factors, and cross multiplying in the module "Why Cross Multiply?"

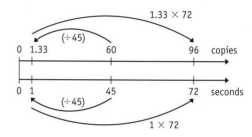

During the discussion, be sure to raise the issue of whether or not the double number lines have to be labeled by consecutive integers. Be prepared to discuss the difference between working with scale factors and working with unit rates. (Scale factors are applied to enlarge or reduce units; unit rates find the rate for one unit.) For additional practice, assign the *Double Number Lines* reproducible on page A31 in the appendix. Discuss the students' solutions and representations. Follow this discussion by having students play the *Find My Matching Value* game, using the reproducible on pages A32–A33. Each time you play this game, the values change and new problems are created.

Meeting Individual Needs

For students who may need more support to reason through the copier problem, present additional data points on the double number line. Some students may wish to represent these values in a table while others may need to focus on the scale-factor strategy, seeing it modeled several times.

For students ready for a challenge, set up the unit labels as seconds but ask how many copies can be made in two minutes.

REFERENCE/FURTHER READING

Piper, Lisa, Nancy Marchand-Martella, and Ronald Martella. 2010. "Use of Explicit Instruction and Double-Dosing to Teach Ratios, Proportions, and Percentages to At-Risk Middle School Students." *Journal of At-Risk Issues* 15 (2): 9–17.

Mathematical Focus

- (6.RP.3) Use ratio and rate reasoning to solve real-world and mathematical problems.
- (7.RP.2d) Explain what a point (x, y) on the graph of a proportional relationship means in terms of the situation, with special attention to the points $(0, 0)$ and $(1, r)$ where r is the unit rate.

Potential Challenges and Misconceptions

Many students are unaware that there are various appropriate representations for modeling rate of change. In addition to double number lines, tape diagrams, and tables, the coordinate plane is an appropriate model. The greatest challenge students have with graphing on the Cartesian plane is determining which is the independent variable and which is the dependent variable. Students need multiple opportunities with various situations in order to develop an understanding of which axis represents which variable. You may want to encourage your students to ask the question, "Does *this* depend on *that*?" Comparing distance traveled over time is a good starting point since students can ask the question, "Does the distance depend on the time, or does the time depend on the distance?" It is also important to include situations where the starting point is not at $(0, 0)$.

In the Classroom

It is always interesting to think about how fast or how slow certain animals move. Two representations that are extremely effective in comparing various rates are the double number line and the coordinate plane. Before working with the coordinate plane, it is important to determine what your students know about the relationship between the x- and y-axes and how the intervals on each axis are determined. For instance, in science there is emphasis on the fact that the x-axis is the independent axis and can stand alone. Think about time, for example. Time is independent, is continuous, and does not depend on any other factors. On the other hand, a dependent variable, or a variable represented on the y-axis, changes based upon the independent variable. The distance something travels depends on the amount of time it has been moving.

Pose the following problem situation and ask the students what the independent variable is and what the dependent variable is.

> A rabbit hops 3 feet in 4 seconds. At this rate, how far will it hop in 16 seconds?

Next, have students find the scale and unit factors associated with this relationship. Then tell them to graph the relationship.

Hand out the *Snail on the Move* reproducible on page A34 of the appendix and ask students to solve the problems, which involve inches and minutes (see below). Notice that the reproducible includes a graph and a double number line. Observe which students choose to begin with the graph and which begin with the double number line. This will provide information about which representation individual students prefer and with which ones they may need more practice.

> If a snail travels 3 inches in 8 minutes, how far will it travel in 1 minute? How far will this snail travel in 15 minutes if the snail continues at the same rate of speed?

Again, ask the students to identify the unit rate and scale factor and where they can be found in the representations.

As the students are working, pay close attention to how they label the axes. Some students will label the y-axis "Time in Minutes," while others will label the x-axis "Time in Minutes." Challenge those students who label the y-axis "Time" to think about whether the time depends on the distance or the distance depends on the time.

After an allotted period of time, ask student volunteers to share their solutions. At the conclusion of the discussion, assign the problems from the *How Far Might They Travel?* reproducible on page A35 of the appendix.

Meeting Individual Needs

For students who struggle with the snail questions, have them solve a simpler problem first by changing the ratio in the first question to 3:12 and asking about 20 minutes in the second question. However, for students needing more of a challenge, you might eliminate the question about the unit rate and move directly to the second question: *How far will this snail travel in 15 minutes?* Or, add a third question focusing on a different component, such as *How long might it take the snail to travel $9\frac{1}{2}$ inches?*

REFERENCE/FURTHER READING

Noyce Foundation. 2013. Inside Mathematics. http://insidemathematics.org/common-core-math-tasks/6th-grade/6-2008%20Snail%20Pace.pdf.

Mathematical Focus

- (7.RP.2) Recognize and represent proportional relationships between quantities.
- (7.RP.2a) Decide whether two quantities are in a proportional relationship.
- (7.G.A.1) Solve problems involving scale drawings of geometric figures, including computing actual lengths and areas from a scale drawing and reproducing a scale drawing at a different scale.

Potential Challenges and Misconceptions

Within textbook problems, students' exposure is often limited to "nice" numbers with ratios or scale factors provided, which is not the case when applying mathematical ideas to real-world data. When confronted with the latter, many students do not know how to proceed. Making comparisons between a typical chair and scaled versions of that chair is a strategic way for students to develop an understanding of how an object can be dilated—that is, enlarged or reduced—by given scale factors, and how to determine such data in real-world settings.

In the Classroom

One teacher provides her students with pictures of a child, Emma, sitting on three different-size chairs, all of which are proportional; the ratio of the large to the middle chair is the same as that of the middle chair to the small chair. (See *Giant and Tiny Chairs* on pages A36–A37.) Before she challenges them to use the pictures and Emma's measurements to discover how tall each of the three chairs is, she goes over the measurements that are given to ensure the students understand what a sit measurement is, where the top of Emma's boots are, and what constitutes the height of the chairs. This teacher suggests the students work in pairs and agree on how to begin. She also suggests that each student take his or her own measurements (using a standard ruler) as a means of double-checking the work.

As she walks around the class, this teacher notices some students really struggling to determine how to go about solving the problem. Rather than let them struggle to the point of frustration or quitting, she brings the class back together, even though the students are not finished answering all the questions. She suggests that it might be helpful if some student volunteers share their *strategies* (not answers). She does this often to ensure that even students who may struggle have an opportunity to choose among strategies others are using and that are effective for solving these problems. She begins this sharing by asking Marissa and her partner how they worked on the problem. Marissa explains, "I started by finding the length and width of the medium-size chair and multiplied that length and width to find the surface area of the seat." As soon as Marissa makes that statement, many of the other students agree that they did the same thing.

Next, the teacher asks Nicole and Tyler to share what they've done. These partners project a table they have made to organize their work. Nicole explains that she kept getting confused by the ratios and the scale factors, so they made the table to help them organize their data.

Tucker then volunteers to explain how he is determining the heights of the chairs. He reports, "I measured the biggest chair by measuring from the top of the chair to the seat, and I will compare it to Emma's height."

This teacher then encourages the students to choose one of the shared strategies if they've been struggling or to finish their calculations if they already have a method that is working for them.

Meeting Individual Needs

For students who need more support, it may be helpful to enlarge the pictures and break the problem down into different components. Have them do all the measuring and record the measurements in a table. After that is finished, suggest they find the ratio between the normal-size chair and the largest chair, followed by the ratio between the normal-size chair and the smallest chair. Keep in mind that if the students begin with the smallest chair and work their way to the largest chair, the scale factors will be whole numbers, but if they work their way from the largest to the smallest, the scale factors will be fractions.

REFERENCE/FURTHER READING

Van de Walle, John, Jennifer Bay-Williams, LouAnn Lovin, and Karen Karp. 2013. *Teaching Student-Centered Mathematics: Developmentally Appropriate Instruction for Grades 6–8.* 2d ed. New York: Pearson.

Mathematical Focus
- (7.RP.2) Recognize and represent proportional relationships between quantities.
- (7.RP.2a) Decide whether two quantities are in a proportional relationship.

Potential Challenges and Misconceptions

Many students neglect to think about whether the comparisons they make are proportional or not because they typically are not challenged to do so in contextual situations. In mathematics, students are often given tables that progress by consecutive values in the input column and proportional values in the output column. This means there is little need to test for proportionality until or unless students work with similar figures in geometry. Until students have a need to test for proportionality, they are unlikely to realize that there are different ways of testing for it.

In the Classroom

The ratio and proportional reasoning standards expect students to identify proportional relationships within contextual situations as well as in mathematical presentations. These mathematical situations may be presented as values in a table, ordered pairs on a coordinate plane, polygonal figures that have the same general shape but are different sizes, and equations. Most students enjoy working with similar figures in geometric settings. Project the shapes from the *Class Starter for Am I Proportional?* reproducible on page A38 in the appendix and distribute copies of the reproducible to students. Challenge them to experiment with ways in which they might determine whether or not the rectangles are proportional. Before they begin their investigations, ask the students to make predictions about which of the figures are proportional and which ones are not based upon visual inspection. Be sure they record their predictions. As the students play around with determining which shapes are proportional, walk around the classroom and listen to the language they use as they compare the figures. Some students will simply make a guess while others may measure the lengths and widths, write ratios, and simplify those ratios to see if they are equivalent. If the ratios are equivalent, the shapes are proportional. Other students may draw a diagonal from the origin through the opposite vertex and identify those rectangles that share the same diagonal. Students who have experience with graphing ratios will recognize that all the points on the diagonal are equivalent and, therefore, the figures that share the same diagonal are proportional. This is an important concept that you should emphasize during the class discussion.

After discussing the ways in which to test for proportional rectangles, project the tables from the same reproducible. Again challenge the students to identify which of the tables are proportional.

Notice that the tables do not increase by consecutive values, so students need to actually test the ratios to determine if they are equivalent and therefore proportional to one another. After an allotted period of time, invite student volunteers to share their reasoning. Notice that as the students justify their reasoning, most will no longer be talking about adding the same amount but rather will be discussing multiples. This is an important leap for students to make.

The next representation to think about is whether or not ordered pairs for a figure and its image are proportional. Propose that your students graph the ordered pairs (3, 5), (6, 5), (3, 10) and (6, 10) and ask them to predict whether or not they will have a proportional image if they take each of the (x, y) values and dilate them by applying $(3x, y)$ to each ordered pair. Discuss the results and point out that the figure is skewed and is not proportional. Next, ask them to predict what will happen if they take each of the original points and dilate them by applying $(0.5x, 0.5y)$. Discuss how the image compares to the original figure. Finally, ask them to apply $(2x + 3, 2y + 6)$. Notice on this image that the shape will be proportional but the figure will be translated. After these discussions, assign the *Am I Proportional?* reproducible on page A39 in the appendix.

Meeting Individual Needs

When grouping students for these explorations, think about pairing students of the same ability level together so all students have an opportunity to share their thinking. In one class we observed students relying on the most articulate student in their group of six, which meant the other five students were not thinking or reasoning through the representations. Groups of three or four tend to work best.

REFERENCE/FURTHER READING
Reif, Dan. 2006. "Mathematical Lens: House, Amherst, Massachusetts." *Mathematics Teacher* 100 (1): 26–29.

Mathematical Focus

- (6.RP.3) Use ratio and rate reasoning to solve real-world and mathematical problems.
- (7.RP.2c) Represent proportional relationships by equations.

Potential Challenges and Misconceptions

Ask almost any student how he or she might solve a proportion, and inevitably the student will reply, "Cross multiply." If you follow up that first question with "Why does cross multiplying work?" most students will say, "I don't know." There is no question that an efficient way to solve proportional problems involving missing values is to set up a proportion and cross multiply; however, it is crucial that students understand why cross multiplication works so they will be reasoning rather than following a blind procedure. Rather than just show students how to cross multiply, it is far more beneficial to break up the process into steps that relate to the previous work students have done with finding scale factors and unit rates.

In the Classroom

One teacher begins by projecting the following problem on the board for her students to solve using any strategy they like.

> There are 210 calories in 10 candy kisses. At this rate, how many calories are in 36 candy kisses?

After an allotted period of time, this teacher invites student volunteers to share their strategies and solutions. Not surprisingly, some say they used a scale factor, some report using a unit rate, and one student explains that she cross multiplied. Before engaging in a class discussion, this teacher posts samples of the three ways in which the students solved the problem (see figure).

Scale Factor	Unit Rate	Cross Multiplication
$\frac{210 \text{ calories}}{10 \text{ kisses}} = \frac{c \text{ calories}}{36 \text{ kisses}}$	$\frac{210 \text{ calories}}{10 \text{ kisses}}$	$\frac{210 \text{ calories}}{10 \text{ kisses}} = \frac{c \text{ calories}}{36 \text{ kisses}}$
$\frac{210 \times 3.6}{10 \times 3.6} = \frac{756}{36}$	$\rightarrow 21 \text{ calories} / 1 \text{ kiss}$	$10c = 210 \times 36$ $c = \frac{210 \times 36}{10}$
$210 \times 3.6 = 756 \text{ calories}$	$21 \times 36 = 756 \text{ calories}$	$c = 21 \times 36 = 756 \text{ calories}$

Bonnie explains that she set up a proportion and found the scale factor between 10 kisses and 36 kisses is 3.6 since 10 × 3.6 equals 36, and she multiplied 210 × 3.6 to make the proportion equivalent. The teacher asks Bonnie what property she is using when she multiplies both the 10 and the 210 by 3.6. After a brief moment, Bonnie exclaims that she is using the multiplicative identity property and is actually multiplying by 1.

Next, the teacher invites D'Wann to explain his work. He tells the class that he likes finding the unit rate. He explains that he divided the 210 calories by the 10 candy kisses to find how many calories there were in 1 candy kiss. He then explains that when he knew the unit rate was 21 calories per candy kiss, he used that rate to multiply by the 36 candy kisses to find the total number of calories in 36 candy kisses.

Maddie shares her cross multiplication and says it is a shortcut her brother showed her. The teacher asks her to talk the class through the steps she used and to see if she and the class can relate those steps to the scale factor and unit rate models. Maddie agrees and says that she multiplied the 10 kisses by the unknown calories and then multiplied the 36 kisses by the 210 calories to write her equation. Then to solve the equation, she explains, she divided both sides by 10. As she is speaking, many students raise their hands, wanting to make connections. Before she calls on other students, the teacher asks Maddie if she can see any similarities among the three methods. Maddie agrees that the three procedures all include multiplication and division, but the order in which they do the computation is different. Then the teacher asks the class if anyone wants to add other observations, and Skylar remarks that the order in which the computation is done does not matter, since in multiplication the commutative property works. She adds that when she solves the equation $10c = 210(36)$ she doesn't divide by 10 but rather multiplies by the reciprocal of 10, so her work $(\frac{1}{10})10c = 210(36)(\frac{1}{10})$ is really the same as both the scale factor and the unit rate methods. The teacher summarizes what Skylar has shared, emphasizing the fact that all three methods are mathematically correct and they, the students, should use whichever strategy makes the most sense to them.

Finally, the teacher assigns the *Human Proportions* reproducible on page A40 in the appendix to engage her students in investigating some proportions in their own bodies and allows the students to use whatever strategies they want.

Meeting Individual Needs

Encourage students who do not understand why they are cross multiplying to use ratio tables, unit rates, or scale factors, rather than rely on a procedure that does not make sense to them. Some students may be able to develop their understanding over time, so it is helpful to post the different ways of solving a proportion so the options are available to all students as they work to make sense of cross multiplying.

REFERENCE/FURTHER READING

Cohen, Jessica. 2013. "Strip Diagrams: Illuminating Proportions." *Mathematics Teaching in the Middle School* 18 (9): 536–42.

Mathematical Focus

- (6.RP.3d) Use ratio reasoning to convert measurement units; manipulate and transform units appropriately when multiplying or dividing quantities.
- (7.RP.1) Compute unit rates associated with ratios of fractions, including ratios of lengths, areas and other quantities measured in like or different units.
- (7.RP.2c) Represent proportional relationships by equations.

Potential Challenges and Misconceptions

With today's ever more global society, students must learn to make conversions between various units such as miles and kilometers, Celsius and Fahrenheit, and US currency and pesos, Canadian dollars, the English pound, and the Euro. They must also make conversions between US units, such as minutes and hours, feet and miles, and feet and yards. One of the greatest confusions students (and many adults) experience is determining whether to multiply or divide when making the conversions.

In the Classroom

Providing a comprehensive mathematics project for a fictitious trip a family might take is an interesting way in which to engage your students in the reasoning and sense making that is being demanded of them. This module outlines a simulated trip that a family might make while traveling cross-country. Our family starts out in New England, travels across the Trans-Canada Highway, and drives back across the northern states as it goes from Boston to Seattle. However, before assigning the logistics for the trip and the mathematics that the students will compute, it is important to ensure that the students have developed the necessary proficiencies.

Begin by projecting the activators from the *Class Starter for Vacation Travels* reproducible on page A41 in the appendix. Tell the students they need to determine how many miles there are between Norwood, Massachusetts, and Montreal, Quebec, Canada, and about how long it will take a family to drive that distance if it averages 65 miles per hour on that leg of the trip and does not stop for food or fuel (325 miles; 5 hours). After a short period of time in which the students calculate their responses, direct each of them to compare their answers with a partner's answer and if they disagree to try to convince their partner they are correct. After giving students a chance to discuss their answers in pairs, ask student volunteers to share their answers and, more importantly, how they calculated the solutions.

Next project the question relating to the conversion of US dollars to Canadian dollars. The students must determine how many US dollars ($160) were exchanged at a rate of $1.02 for the $163.20 Canadian Courtney received. Because the rates between the US and Canadian dollars in 2013 are almost equivalent, this may not excite your students. Share the fact that in 2009 the rate of exchange was $1.26 Canadian to the US dollar, and challenge your students to determine the difference in the amount of Canadian money Courtney would have received in 2009 versus 2013 ($201.60 − $163.20 = $38.40). Invite a student volunteer to share the solution after each student has had an opportunity to compare his or her solution with a partner's and convince the partner that his or her answer is correct.

Follow this discussion by projecting the third problem, and allow time for your students to determine the miles they could travel in 4 hours and the number of gallons of the car would use if they traveled 390 miles in 6 hours and used 15 gallons of gas (260 miles; 10 gallons). Based on this information, students will also determine how far they might have traveled on 150 gallons of gas. Individual students often rely on one technique without first looking at the numbers involved. As a result, students who always tend to find unit rates may miss the friendliness of the numbers 4 and 6. If they did not do so, ask them how they could use that information to find the missing value for miles or gallons ($\frac{2}{3}$ of 390 is 260, and $\frac{2}{3}$ of 15 is 10).

To provide students with the opportunity to grapple with ratios involving numbers less than one, project the following scenario:

Tim can walk $\frac{1}{2}$ mile in $\frac{1}{4}$ hour. At this rate, how far can Tim walk in an hour?

Walk around and listen as the students discuss how to work with the complex fraction $\frac{\frac{1}{2}}{\frac{1}{4}}$. Note those students who revert to additive thinking, counting by halves, rather than dividing. Think about how you might guide the students to relate this to other problems they have solved. You might ask, *How many fourths are there in one-half?* After this discussion, assign the *Vacation Travels* reproducible on page A42 in the appendix.

Meeting Individual Needs

For a challenge, ask your students to determine how many miles per hour their car is traveling if the speedometer reads 121 kilometers per hour. Students should be able to determine that since there is about 0.62 kilometer in 1 mile, there is also 0.62 km/hr. in 1 mi./hr. If any of your students grew up in countries that use the metric system, this would be an opportunity to recognize their knowledge. You may wish to give them the chance to support others.

REFERENCE/FURTHER READING

Langrall, Cynthia, and Jane Swafford. 2000. "Three Balloons for Two Dollars: Developing Proportional Reasoning." *Mathematics Teaching in the Middle School* 6 (4): 254–61.

Mathematical Focus

- (6.RP.3d) Use ratio reasoning to convert measurement units.
- (7.RP.1) Compute unit rates associated with ratios of fractions, including ratios of lengths, areas, and other quantities measured in like or different units.
- (7.RP.3) Use proportional relationships to solve multistep ratio and percent problems.

Potential Challenges and Misconceptions

Posing problems is one of the more difficult cognitive demands we place on students. It requires that students understand mathematics and related contexts. They must also be able to predict solution strategies and determine whether there is one or multiple answers. Students typically have few experiences with posing problems and yet the ability to recognize potential questions to ask about a situation is key to recognizing that mathematics is useful to them. For instance, when shopping, students may be faced with deciding whether 20 percent of the regular price for a backpack is a better deal than using a coupon for $5.00 off. If we are to empower students to reason through situations like this, we need to engage students in creating their own problems. One way to support students' ability to pose problems is to offer them problem starters. Problem starters might include answers, contexts, equations or computations, data, or representations. Experiences with each of these types of problem starters will help students deepen their understanding of the domain and gain appreciation of its usefulness.

In the Classroom

Ask your students if any of them look at advertisements in the newspaper, store circulars that come in the mail, or Internet ads. Follow this question by asking whether they would save more money by buying a new leather jacket if it was on sale at 30 percent off or by using a coupon that offered $30 off. Provide an allotted period of time for the students to talk about this question. Discuss their responses and emphasize that in this case it depends on the original cost. Suggest this as an example of decisions they must make whenever they go shopping. Then begin the activity by asking if any of the students have ever played Jeopardy, and ask those who have to describe how the contestants respond with a question. Explain that they will be doing something similar in that they will be given information and must respond with a problem statement and question. Begin by saying, "The answer is $4.75 per box. What is the problem?" Have students work in small groups to compose their problems and then share them. During the class discussion, ask questions like, *What is the same about these problems? What is different? What solution strategies might you use to solve them?*

Then display the proportion $\frac{5}{12} = \frac{n}{108}$ and challenge your students to pose a problem that might be solved using this proportion.

After an allotted period of time, invite student volunteers to share their story problems. For example:

> Danny scores 5 baskets for every 12 attempts he takes. How many baskets will he make at this same rate if he makes 108 attempts?
>
> Harry reads 5 pages in 12 minutes; at this rate how many pages will he read in 108 minutes?

Copy and cut out the five cards in the *Problem Starters* reproducible on page A43, distribute them to five working areas in your classroom, and divide students among the areas. Students at each area, working in pairs, should spend an allotted period of time writing a problem that meets the criteria. Then students should rotate clockwise to a different area. Continue until students have written problems for each of the starters. Collect the problems and check them for appropriateness. Choose ones to provide as responses to each starter. Write these on easel paper to create a gallery walk. You may choose to ask students to solve the problems, identify those they would solve with a unit-rate, scale-factor, or cross-multiplication approach, and/or make one positive comment about each problem and ask one question about the problem or the solution method. Upon completion, assign the *Creating Problems* reproducible on page A44.

You or students can create similar problem starters so that the activity can be repeated. It may also be helpful to connect with your colleagues to determine what the students are studying in their other subject areas. Making connections across classes can be quite satisfying to students and bring a mathematical lens to their understanding of, for example, historical events.

Meeting Individual Needs

Posing problems is extremely challenging for many students. Since they are working with proportions, be sure that if students struggle with a context, you pose questions such as, *What rates might you compare? Are you thinking about how many times you can complete an activity in a given time period? Did you think about distance compared with time? Or speed compared with time? Or the number of kilometers in a given number of miles?*

REFERENCE/FURTHER READING

Chapin, Suzanne, and Nancy Anderson. 2003. "Crossing the Bridge to Formal Proportional Reasoning." *Mathematics Teaching in the Middle School* 8 (8): 420–23.

Converting Ratios to Percents

Mathematical Focus

- (6.RP.3c) Find a percent of a quantity as a rate per 100 (e.g., 30% of a quantity means 30/100 times the quantity); solve problems involving finding the whole, given a part and the percent.

Potential Challenges and Misconceptions

When told to convert ratios to percents, many students immediately set up a proportion and cross multiply. Although this approach works, most students do not understand why it works or how the percent is related to the ratio. Engaging students in representing a ratio on a hundreds grid is an effective way of developing an understanding of the relationship between a given ratio and its corresponding percent.

In the Classroom

One teacher distributes 10-by-10 grids to her students. She asks the students what number they might write to represent just 1 of the 100 squares. The students typically respond $\frac{1}{100}$ or 0.01 or 1%. If no one suggests 1%, she tells or reminds them that 1 square can also be represented by 1%, as *percent* means out of 100. The teacher then invites them to fill in the grid to illustrate how the ratio 3:5 might look. She circles the room as the students work, prodding them when necessary to remember that 3:5 can be thought of as 3 out of 5. She notices two different representations, both of which accurately depict 60 percent.

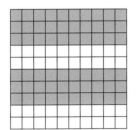 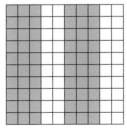

She has a student share each of the diagrams and asks the class, "Where do you *see* three out of five on this grid?" Then she asks her students what percent of the squares are shaded, and they respond with 60 percent. She records on the board:

$$\frac{3}{5} = \frac{60}{100} = 0.60 = 60\%$$

Next she displays a new grid and works with students to model how the ratio 3:8 would look. Students also have new grids to record the representation and some notes. This representation is more challenging because eight is not a factor of one hundred, which means the remainder of four must be accounted for in the diagram. Together the class decides that three of the first eight rows can be shaded. Next the teacher asks, "Is there somewhere else we could shade three out of eight?" They decide to shade the first three squares of the last two rows, leaving four squares. The teacher says, "We have four squares left. I am going to divide them each in half so that there are eight halves. How many should I shade?" Students respond that she should shade in three half squares. Students conclude that 3:8 is the same as $37\frac{1}{2}$ percent. She then gives students time to work in pairs to make notes about the steps they followed to show 3:8.

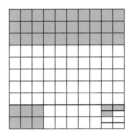

Finally, the teacher assigns the *Show It on the Grid* activity on pages A45–46 in the appendix.

Meeting Individual Needs

For students who need a challenge, ask them to set up a proportion and use multiplicative reasoning between the ratio on the left and its corresponding percent. For instance, given the problem *Sixteen is what percent of 20?*, the student might set up the proportion $\frac{16}{20} = \frac{n}{100}$. Notice the factor between the denominators 20 and 100 is 5, so the missing percent is 16×5, or 80 percent. Be sure the students recognize they are using the multiplicative identity when they multiply both the numerator and the denominator by 5.

REFERENCE/FURTHER READING

Ercole, Leslie K., Marny Frantz, and George Ashline. 2011. "Multiple Ways to Solve Proportions." *Teaching Mathematics in the Middle School* 16 (8): 482–85.

Mathematical Focus

- (6.RP.3c) Find a percent of a quantity as a rate per 100 (e.g., 30% of a quantity means $\frac{30}{100}$ times the quantity); solve problems involving finding the whole, given a part and the percent.

Potential Challenges and Misconceptions

Students who are comfortable with composing and decomposing whole numbers to compute may not realize that they can also apply these techniques to percents. Students who reason about benchmark percents such as 10, 25, 50, 75, and 100 tend to understand percents more deeply and to develop flexible strategies that are helpful in real-world situations. For instance, 45% is equivalent to 50% − 5% or 20% + 25%. One method that helps students successfully find a percent of a number is to use tables, but that requires students to understand that 100 percent is equal to 1 or 1 whole.

In the Classroom

As students can forget or never really understand that 100 percent is the same as one whole, one teacher displays a 10-by-10 grid and reestablishes that one square is $\frac{1}{100}$, or 1 percent. She then asks about ninety-nine squares, and once students identify $\frac{99}{100}$ and 99 percent, she asks about one hundred squares. When they respond, she records $\frac{100}{100} = 100\% = 1$.

Then she asks students what 50 percent of ten might be. Sadia says, "It's five because 50 percent is just like one-half." Then the teacher asks about 20 percent of ten. Mila responds, "I find it easy to think about 10 percent. Ten percent of ten is one, so 20 percent is twice that, or two." Then she asks students to think about the number forty and work in pairs to list percents they can identify easily. After an allotted amount of time, she asks students to report the percents they found and how they found them. Most students say they found 5 percent, 10 percent, 20 percent, 50 percent, and 75 percent. She reminds students that they also know 100 percent. The teacher then tells students that she wants them to apply this good reasoning to more challenging problems.

She gives students copies of the *Percent Templates* reproducible on page A47 in the appendix and tells them to use the tables to think about how they can use percents they know to find other percents. She asks them to find 35 percent of 120 but first establishes that 120 is the given value, and because it's the whole, it represents

Given Value 120	Percent 100
30 ÷4	25 ÷4
12 ÷10	10 ÷10
(42)	35

Given Value 120	Percent 100
12₿	10
24	20
6	5
42	35

100 percent. The figures at the bottom of the first column show how two of the sixth-grade students calculate 35 percent of 120 using percent tables.

Notice that the first student has used the values of 25 percent and 10 percent in the table while the second student has used the values of 10 percent, 20 percent, and 5 percent. During a class discussion, the first student explains that she knew the value was between 25 percent and 50 percent and that she could see that if 25 + 10 = 35 then 25% + 10% = 35%. The second student shares that he likes doubling and halving. Both of these students show confidence in decomposing numbers. She then challenges the students to find 23% of $80, 62% of $240, and 125% of $40.

After discussing the various ways of finding percents, which might include using one-fourth for 25 percent or one-fifth for 20 percent, the teachers asks the students to pair up and complete the *Percent Card Sort* activity on pages A48–A49 in the appendix.

Meeting Individual Needs

For students who need more support, it is helpful to provide them with percent tables where some of the benchmark percents are already included and ask them to find the missing values, for example 10 percent, 5 percent, and 1 percent. A scaffolded table for the problem *What is 45% of 160?* might look like the following:

Value	Percent
160	
	50
	45
16	10
8	

For students who need a challenge, direct them to find an equation that best represents what happens algebraically when finding the percent of a given value. For example, $0.35 \times 120 = 42$ or, more generally, *percent × whole = part*. You might also challenge these students to determine which would be the better buy: an item on sale for 40% off its original price or an item on sale for 15% off combined with a coupon for an additional 25% off. (Most students will respond that the item will cost the same instead of realizing that the 15% off is calculated first, followed by an additional 25% off.)

REFERENCE/FURTHER READING

Collins, Anne, and Linda Dacey. 2010. *Zeroing in on Number and Operations: Key Ideas and Misconceptions, Grades 7–8.* Portland, ME: Stenhouse.

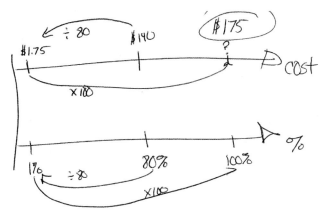

Mathematical Focus

- (6.RP.3c) Find a percent of a quantity as a rate per 100 (e.g., 30% of a quantity means $\frac{30}{100}$ times the quantity); solve problems involving finding the whole, given a part and the percent.

Potential Challenges and Misconceptions

Many students rely on a formula or procedure for finding percents instead of relying on sense making and reasoning, so they struggle when trying to solve problems in which they are given a part and must find the whole. The use of multiple representations and various strategies such as tables, tape diagrams, and double number lines is instrumental in helping students limit their reliance on formulas and cutesy sayings.

In the Classroom

One teacher begins his class by projecting the following problem on the board.

> An advertisement in a sporting goods store states the discounted price of a Super Slick skateboard is now only $140. You pay only 80% of the original cost. How much did the skateboard cost originally?

After an allotted period of time, he calls on different students to share their work.

Mario explains, "We couldn't start at 100 percent 'cause that is what we were looking for, so we left a space for that. We started at 80 percent, then filled in the table and worked backward. We added the cost at 80 percent to the cost at 20 percent to get 100 percent, so we also added the $140 and the $35 to get $175." (See figure.)

Value	Percent
175	100
140	80
70	40
35	20
17.5	10

Julie shares her double number line. She explains, "We knew that 80 percent was equivalent to $140.00, so we divided by 80 to find the unit rate, which was $1.75. Then we multiplied the unit rate by 100 to get the cost for 100 percent." (See figure.)

Next, Zahar shares her tape diagrams. She comments, "One hundred forty dollars is only 80 percent of the whole, so I needed to add 20 percent more. I divided the 80 percent into four parts, so each part is 20 percent. One hundred forty divided by 4 is 35, so each part is worth 35. I multiplied 5 by 35 and got $175." (See figure.)

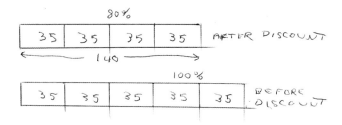

After discussing what they would need to do if instead, the problem stated that Mario used a 20 percent off coupon, this teacher assigns the *Play It Forward* game on pages A50–A51.

Meeting Individual Needs

Some students do best if they are able to master one representation for working with percents and rates. It is highly beneficial for those students to work with either percent tables or double number lines. Either of these representations will enable them to lay a foundation for later mathematics concepts that build on rates and percents.

REFERENCE/FURTHER READING

Common Core Standards Writing Team. 2011. *Progressions for the Common Core State Standards in Mathematics: 6–7, Ratios and Proportional Relationships*. Draft. http://commoncoretools.files.wordpress.com/2012/02/ccss_progression_rp_67_2011_11_12_corrected.pdf.

Mathematical Focus

- (7.RP.3) Use proportional relationships to solve multistep ratio and percent problems. Examples: simple interest, tax, markups and markdowns, gratuities and commissions, fees, percent increase and decrease, percent error.

Potential Challenges and Misconceptions

Determining the tax for an item and figuring the amount of tip to leave for the wait staff are everyday life skills that many students are beginning to realize they need. Students who lack flexible thinking with percents will not be able to compute tips quickly and may overtip or undertip. Accuracy is also important when determining such things as taxes and commissions. This financial literacy will affect your students throughout their lives, so it is important that they develop both precision and flexibility.

In the Classroom

To begin his lesson, one teacher asks his students to use their individual whiteboards to indicate how much money they would leave for a tip if their meal cost thirty dollars. After they record their answers, he tells them to hold up their whiteboards, and he writes the students' responses on the class board. The values vary from one dollar to ten dollars. The teacher asks his students to share their strategies for determining the tip.

Avery offers, "My dad always leaves five dollars, so that is what I think the tip is."

Josh shares, "My mom is a waitress, so we always multiply the total bill by two and move the decimal point one place to the left, so I would leave six dollars."

Jackson adds, "My sister has a card she uses, and she shows the thirty dollars, then decides what percent tip to leave and puts down the amount on the card."

Simon nods his head and adds, "My dad rounds up the amount [of the meal], then divides by three, so he would leave a ten-dollar tip."

After his students report out, this teacher asks them to think individually about why people leave tips before telling the students to turn to their shoulder partners and share ideas.

After an allotted period of time, he asks student volunteers to report their findings. Some students say people leave tips to show they appreciate the service, others say it's because wait staff do not make enough money, and still others say it's because it is expected of them. The teacher discusses the custom of tipping that exists in the United States before asking his students what they know about sales taxes. This teacher also tells them that the customary tip is between 15% and 20%, depending on how good the service is.

He presents the following problem, again having students think individually, share with their partners, and then report their ideas.

> Diego bought a soccer ball that cost $15. The sales tax is 4% in his state. How much was the tax on the soccer ball? ($0.60) How much did he have to pay for the soccer ball? ($15 + $0.60 = $15.60)

Next, he introduces the concept of commissions by explaining that as he was working his way through school, he sold hot dogs at Fenway Park. His salary was only $2.50 per hour, but his commission was 45 percent on hot dogs, which he sold for $1.25 each. His typical workday was four hours, and he sold an average of 235 hot dogs per game. The teacher challenges the students to calculate his commission as well as how much money he made during each ball game (commission: $132.19; salary: $10; total pay: $142.19). He continues his story by telling them he worked eighty-one days per season and asks them how much money he made on average from opening day through the final game of the season (commission for season: $10,707.39; salary per season: $810.00; total pay per season: $11,517.39).

Next he assigns the *Match It and Prove It* activity on pages A52–A53 in the appendix. After students complete the matching activity, you can have them meet in small groups to discuss their work. Ask them to identify problems they found more and less challenging and why they think this was the case. Have them share the techniques they used to prove their choices were correct. Encourage students to note the similarities and differences among their strategies. If no one in the group has used an equation, challenge them to do so.

Meeting Individual Needs

The matching activity can help to relieve anxiety in some students because they know all of the correct answers are given. You may want to make copies of the *Percent Templates* reproducible from page A47 in the appendix available for students who would benefit from this organizational structure.

REFERENCE/FURTHER READINGS

Ercole, Leslie K., Marny Franz, and George Ashline. 2011. "Multiple Ways to Solve Proportions." *Mathematics Teaching in the Middle School* 16 (8): 482–90.

Mathematical Focus

- (7.RP.3) Use proportional relationships to solve multistep ratio and percent problems. Examples: simple interest, tax, markups and markdowns, gratuities and commissions, fees, percent increase and decrease, percent error.

Potential Challenges and Misconceptions

It is important for students to grapple with the application of percents, and students often find problems involving a percent increase challenging because they are unfamiliar with the language. Their success rate will improve if they have the opportunity to see a variety of solution techniques. It is important to expose students to solutions involving tables, double number lines, tape diagrams, and equations so that they can make connections among the representations and determine which is best for their use. Introducing new applications is also an opportunity to review multiple representations while connecting them to equations.

In the Classroom

In one classroom, the teacher introduces the application of double number lines by asking his students how they might represent 25 percent of seventy-six dollars on the double number lines. He allots about three minutes for the students to make their notations before telling them to turn to their shoulder partners and discuss their diagrams, samples of which are shown below.

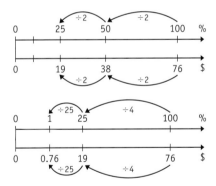

As he listens to the conversations, he is confident that the students are comfortable with using double number lines and with the concept of finding percents. He moves on to discussing percent of increase. He begins this segment of the lesson by asking his students why they think the cost of something increases. He then asks, "How could we use our double number lines to find what something would cost if its original price of seventy-six dollars were increased by 25 percent?" The students quickly (and happily) realize that they merely need to add nineteen dollars to seventy-five dollars to find the increased price of ninety-four dollars.

Because this teacher knows students are expected to summarize their thinking on tests, he introduces the value of writing a "written model" for the equation. He describes a written model as an equation in which only the key words and operators are identified in either an equation or an expression. He invites his students to help him write a written model for the problem they have just solved. Together they identify the model: *original price × percent of increase + original price = total cost.* He asks Ming to come to the document camera to substitute in numerical values to check the solution to the equation with the double number lines. Ming writes $76 × 25\% + $76 = T. She solves it as $19 + $76 = $94, which matches their previous work.

Following this discussion, the teacher assigns two problems, which he projects on his whiteboard (see the *Increase Problems* reproducible on page A54 in the appendix). The second problem is best solved algebraically. Following the construction of the written model, the students substitute in the numerical values and solve the problem. The teacher also reminds them to define the variables they are using to help a reader understand the equation.

After an allotted period of time, he invites student volunteers to report their solutions and representations to the first problem. Their representations include the following:

Value	Percent
55	100
27.50	50
−2.75	−5
24.75	45
79.75	145

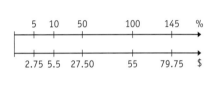

Then students discuss the second problem. Henry shares his written model: *original cost + 20%(original cost) = $768.* The teacher asks if anyone has anything different. Bennett shares his equation: *0.20(original cost) + original cost = $768.* He explains that they can't multiply by a percent. The teacher then challenges the students to solve the problem using c for cost. Henry shares his solution, which is $1.20c = 768, or $c = 640. Henry explains the original cost was $640, and the amount of increase was $128.

The class discusses the results of the student work before beginning the problems on the *Percent Stories* reproducible (see page A55 in the appendix).

Meeting Individual Needs

For students who need more scaffolding to solve these problems, you might label the double number lines for the first few problems you assign. As the students become more familiar with the model, you might provide double number lines with appropriate tick marks but allow the students to fill in the values. For students ready for a challenge, ask them to determine equations they might use to find the solutions to the problems and to check their equations using either double number lines or percent tables.

REFERENCE/FURTHER READING

Cohen, Jessica S. 2013. "Strip Diagrams: Illuminating Proportions." *Teaching Mathematics in the Middle School* 18 (9): 536–39.

Percent of Decrease

Mathematical Focus

- (7.RP.3) Use proportional relationships to solve multistep ratio and percent problems. Examples: simple interest, tax, markups and markdowns, gratuities and commissions, fees, percent increase and decrease, percent error.

Potential Challenges and Misconceptions

Many students find percent of decrease problems are the most difficult percent problems to solve. Students become very confused about which values are being compared. Many forget that they must first find the amount of decrease from the original price, and it is that difference that is represented by the percent. The use of tape diagrams, double number lines, and percent tables enables students to develop and demonstrate an understanding of the mathematics involved in working with percents of decrease.

In the Classroom

As with other percent problems, students must develop flexibility in solving percent of decrease problems when given the percent of decrease and the original amount, the amount of decrease and the percent of decrease, or the amount of decrease and the original amount. It is desirable for students to be able to use multiple strategies, but it is most important that every student have one or two with which he or she can demonstrate proficiency and that the student can understand deeply. To encourage this, project the following problem and challenge pairs of students to solve it using any strategy they would like. Tell them to be sure to include a written model for any equations they use.

> The school store netted $2,300 in September, but the amount of money the school store made in October decreased by 15%. What was the amount of decrease? ($345) How much money did the school store make in October? ($1,955)

Provide easel-size paper to each pair of students, and after an appropriate period of time, instruct the students to hang their easel papers around the room. Designate certain areas for students to hang their work depending on the strategy they used. Cluster together the tables, the tape diagrams, the double number lines, and the equation work. Tell your students to compare the solutions within clusters for similarities and differences. After students have had time to do so, invite volunteers to explain how they solved the problem and how or why their strategies are the same as or different from other solutions in the same cluster. Ask questions such as, *How might you define your written model?* (original amount − original amount × percent of decrease = amount made in October) *What shows the original whole?* and *What shows that there was a decrease?*

Follow this discussion by posing a second problem that typically does have a range of responses.

> In December, the school store netted $1,850. In January, it made only $1,275. About what was the percent of decrease? (31%)

Repeat the same process as before: have pairs of students record their solutions on easel paper and hang them in strategy clusters, allow time for students to compare similarities and differences, and discuss the solutions and strategies. Choose one example of each strategy and invite a student volunteer to explain what the representation means and justify the solution. Again, ask about the whole and the discount.

For students who insist on setting up a proportion rather than a linear equation, be sure they understand the necessity of relating the amount of decrease to the percent of decrease and relating the original amount to 100 percent. For the second problem, ask, "Can we use $\frac{1,275}{1,850} = \frac{p}{100}$ to find the solution? Why or why not?"

After completing the discussion, play the *Percent Math-O* game on pages A56–A58 in the appendix.

Meeting Individual Needs

Students who make errors when using proportional representations will most likely experience success when developing written models and then substituting in numerical values to solve percent increase and percent decrease problems. Direct these students to always begin with the written model before they start writing numerical equations. This strategy allows them to solve for the unknown wherever it appears in the equation.

REFERENCE/FURTHER READING

Reys, Robert, and Rustin Reys. 2011. "Mathematics, Anyone?" *Mathematics Teaching in the Middle School* 17 (2): 80–86.

Mathematical Focus

- (6.RP.3) Use ratio reasoning to solve real-world and mathematical problems.
- (7.RP.3) Use proportional relationships to solve multistep ratio and percent problems.

Potential Challenges and Misconceptions

When students are provided the opportunity to pose problems, they engage in the type of thinking that mathematicians do (Weiss and Moore-Russo 2012). Yet students are rarely asked to pose problems; rather, they are given word problems that always provide the questions to be answered. As a result, students' understanding of the usefulness of mathematics is limited, as is their ability to recognize real-world problems that could be solved by applying mathematical ideas. Further, some students do not know where to begin when asked to pose a mathematical question. Using mathematical information drawn from newspapers, studies available on the Internet, or news services that are of interest to students can engage them in this process.

In the Classroom

One teacher displays recent statistics she found on the Internet that relate to the ways in which children and teens engage with media. These are a few of the statistics she shares:

- Twenty-eight percent of teens report that they never text their friends.
- About 60 percent of twelve- and thirteen-year-olds have cell phones.
- Among those who are eight to eighteen years old, about one in six spend more than 10.5 hours a day using media.

The teacher begins with the first item and tells the students to think for a moment about what else they would like to know about this piece of information. After a couple of minutes, she encourages students to share their thinking with their neighbors, brainstorm some new ideas, and record their ideas in the form of questions. She also reminds students to make sure they include some mathematical questions in their lists.

When the students share their thinking with the class, it is clear that they want to know more about why these teens do not text. They want to know whether or not they have phones that will allow them to, whether their parents will allow them to, and whether theses teens' friends text. But they do have mathematical questions as well, including the following:

- What percentage of these teens are sixteen years or older?
- About how many teens is this?
- How has this percentage changed in the past five years?
- What is the ratio of students who text to those who don't?
- What is the percentage of adults who text?

Next the teacher assigns the students to groups of four and tells them to choose one of the other pieces of information displayed. They will follow the same process of brainstorming questions, but this time they will have an opportunity during the next couple of days to use the classroom computers, along with their mathematical

knowledge, to help them find further information they need to answer their questions. Each group is assigned a specific day and time when it may use the computers. Groups create a poster to summarize what they found, along with a two-minute oral presentation. The teacher explains that each poster should include the following information:

- The questions identified
- Additional information found to answer the questions
- The mathematics used to find the answers
- The answers to the questions

This teacher also wants students to practice posing word problems. When not working on the computers, students complete the *What's the Problem?* reproducible on page A59 in the appendix.

When ready, students hang their posters around the room. Following a gallery walk, which allows viewers to gain familiarity with the information on the posters, students give their two-minute oral presentations. After the presentations, all students fill out an exit card, responding to these three questions:

- What information did you find most interesting?
- What is one question you have about the mathematics presented today?
- What are two ways you were a helpful member of your group?

Meeting Individual Needs

For extra practice with mathematical information in the news, ask students to examine the daily newspaper or online news sites to find statistical information that suggests further mathematical questions.

When posing word problems, students may find it helpful to change already written problems before writing their own from scratch. For example, if a problem asks for the whole to be identified, students could provide the whole and ask about the percent or the part. Another strategy would be to change the problem context. Such a change would require students to recognize other contexts in which the mathematics would be useful. You may also wish to allow students to work in pairs so that they can talk about their thinking and refine their ideas.

REFERENCES/FURTHER READING

Silver, Edward A. 2013. "Problem-Posing Research in Mathematics Education: Looking Back, Looking Around, and Looking Ahead." *Educational Studies in Mathematics Education* 83 (1): 157–62.

Weiss, Michael K., and Deborah Moore-Russo. 2012. "Thinking Like a Mathematician." *The Mathematics Teacher* 106 (4): 269–73.

Mathematical Focus

- (6.RP.3c) Find a percent of a quantity as a rate per 100 (e.g., 30% of a quantity means $\frac{30}{100}$ times the quantity); solve problems involving finding the whole, given a part and the percent.
- (7.RP.2) Recognize and represent proportional relationships between quantities.

Potential Challenges and Misconceptions

Many students are comfortable with converting ratios to percents when the ratios represent values less than 100 percent but struggle when the ratios are greater than 100 percent. For example, given a situation where there are 25 percent more boys than girls in grade seven, many students are unable to recognize they are actually working with a 5:4 ratio of boys to girls as well as a 9:1 ratio of parts to the whole. As a result, they are unable to solve a problem that relies on such data.

In the Classroom

One teacher gives her seventh-grade students the following problem:

> There are 25% more seventh graders than six graders in the Collins Middle School. If there is a total of 135 students in grades six and seven, how many seventh graders are there?

Many students solve this problem using a tape diagram and working with percents, while others convert the percents to a ratio and model the ratio relationships. Chang shares his work first, explaining, "I thought about the 25 percent more as meaning there must be 125 percent, or five-fourths as many seventh graders as sixth graders. I also thought that if there were the same number of sixth and seventh graders, then I would have 100 percent, so I made a tape diagram to show five 25 percent parts for grade seven and four 25 percent parts for grade six. Then since the total number of students was 135, I figured that I needed to add the 5 to the 4 and divide the 135 by 9 to show how many students were in each section of my tape diagram. One hundred thirty-five divided by 9 equals 15. This means that 15 times 4 equals 60 grade six students, and 15 times 5 equals 75 grade seven students."

Taylor says, "I did it differently. I made a percent table. Some of what I did is like Chang's, but my work looks different. So I know that 25 percent more means, well, I think it means that if 100 percent is the total number of sixth graders then maybe 125 percent is seventh graders. I started with the ratio of 4 to 5, then multiplied by 3 to get 12 to 16 for a total number of students of 28, then multiplied by 5 to get 20 to 25 and added those to get 45 students, then kept multiplying the ratio of 4 to 5 until the sum of the sixth and seventh graders added up to 135. That happened when I had 60 sixth graders and 75 seventh graders. I also noticed

that in the totals when I got to 90, they increased by 9. I got stuck though because my first values didn't fit the pattern. I don't know why."

6th	7th	total
12	16	28
20	25	45
40	50	90
44	55	99
48	60	108
60	75	135

25% more 7th graders then 6th graders
135 total
60 6th graders + 75 7th graders

Notice that Taylor has made an arithmetic error in scaling 4:5 in the first row. Instead of 12:16, the ratio should be 12:15, which explains why her numbers do not work out. Her observation about the increase by 9 is important and could help her find her arithmetic error, since given a ratio of two parts, 4 and 5, the total number of students must be 9 or a multiple of 9, which is true for all but her first total.

Juanita shares her written model next:

> Sixth + seventh = total students. Sixth + (25% × sixth) + sixth = 135. 2.25(sixth) = 135. Sixth = 60. Seventh = 135 − 60, or 75.

After discussing the three methods with the class, the teacher assigns the problem set from the *Solving Problems* reproducible on page A60 in the appendix.

Meeting Individual Needs

This is a very challenging problem, and you may need to guide struggling students. The written model actually takes the wording from the problem and is a clear and articulate strategy to use. The tape diagram is a straightforward visual representation that is excellent to use with those students who benefit from diagrams. The rate table is similar to a logical and sequential guess-and-check method.

Some students' understanding of percents greater than 100 might deepen by thinking about examples where percents greater than 100 would make sense, such as earning 150 percent of what you expected, and examples where they would not make sense, such as losing 150 percent of your savings. Students often enjoy making up nonsensical examples.

REFERENCE/FURTHER READING

Parker, Melanie. 2004. "Reasoning and Working Proportionally with Percent." *Teaching Mathematics in the Middle School* 9 (6): 326–29.

Name: Date:

Name the activities your group performed, record the data for each member of your group, and write a ratio sentence about one of the activities for each student's data.

Student Name: 30 seconds

Number of _____	
Number of _____	

Sentence:

Student Name: 30 seconds

Number of _____	
Number of _____	

Sentence:

Student Name: 30 seconds

Number of _____	
Number of _____	

Sentence:

Student Name: 30 seconds

Number of _____	
Number of _____	

Sentence:

Jamie: Hi, Chris. What's up?

Chris: Oh, lots. You know that I injured my shoulder last week, right? Well, I just finished practice and my batting was great. My fielding was good, too. And you know my pitching; that is always terrific. I think the coach is going to let me pitch tomorrow, which would be the first time in two weeks. Coach wouldn't let me throw at full speed today, but I can tomorrow. It will feel good to be back on the mound for the team. How are you doing?

Jamie: I'm good.

Chris: Are you coming to Friday's game? It's over at Riverton High. It starts at 5:00 p.m., but the team has to get there early, so I get to leave during science. Ms. Chen is pretty good about that, though; she even comes to a lot of the games herself. She gives us notes for what we miss or gives us the homework for the next day. I've heard that some teachers complain a lot when kids miss classes for games. I'm glad I've got Ms. Chen.

Jamie: Yeah, I'm coming.

Chris: Good. I really like to know that my friends are going to be there. I mean, sometimes I get a bit nervous before I throw that first pitch. I always look at the bleachers and try to find someone I know. Once I do, it calms me right down. Maybe it will be your face I will see first this time. So be sure to be smiling. See you around and I'll look for you at the game.

Jamie: Bye.

Name: Date:

1. What situations might you dramatize that would involve a ratio?

    a.

    b.

    c.

    d.

2. Which situation will you choose?

3. What ratio will you dramatize?

4. How many characters will you include? What characteristics will they have?

5. What will make your dramatization interesting?

EQUIVALENT RATIOS

Name: Date:

1. Gracie mixed two different paint colors in the ratio of 2:7 to make her ideal shade. She made the following table to record the ratios of paint colors she thinks will make the same shade for various quantities of paint.

   a. Complete the table for the missing quantities.

   b. Explain your reasoning.

Color A	2	4		24			180	200
Color B	7		35		105	560		

2. Nick is a fantastic baseball player. Over his career, he leads all his teammates in batting average, which compares the number of hits to the number of times the player is up to bat (at bats). If he continued to hit this well, how many hits would he be expected to have in the following number of batting opportunities?

Hits	3	9				81		117
At Bats	4		28	52	76		120	

3. Chris emptied a bag of candies and counted them. He found that there were 30 chocolate candies for every 80 candies. What five other ratios can you write that are equivalent to this ratio of 30:80?

It's All Relative: Key Ideas and Common Misconceptions About Ratio and Proportion, Grades 6–7 by Anne Collins and Linda Dacey. Copyright © 2014. Stenhouse Publishers.   A4

Name: Date:

Use tape diagrams to model or solve the following situations.

1. The ratio of boys to girls on the unicycle club is 4:3.

2. The ratio of boys to girls in the unicycle club is 4:3. There are a total of 56 members of the club. How many are boys? How many are girls? Justify your reasoning.

3. Tim and Steve had some sports cards in the ratio of 7:5. Tim gave Steve 12 cards. If each of them had the same number of sports cards in the end, how many sports cards did Tim have in the beginning? Justify your reasoning.

4. The ratio of scores that Gina, Belle, and Katie got on their mathematics test was 7:10:12. If the total number of points the girls scored was 232, how many points did each girl earn?

Name: Date:

Fill in the missing numbers and complete the sentence to generalize the representation.

1.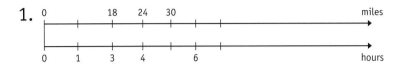

These ratios are all equivalent to _____.

2.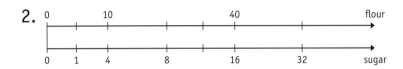

These ratios are all equivalent to _____.

3.

These ratios are all equivalent to _____.

Copy the rulers and slides onto card stock and cut them out. Make slits as indicated by the dashed lines and fit one slide onto each ruler.

Ratio 3:7

0	3	6	9	12	15	18	21	24	27	30	33	36
0	7	14	21	28	35	42	49	56	63	70	77	84

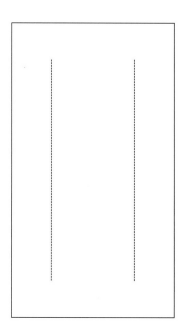 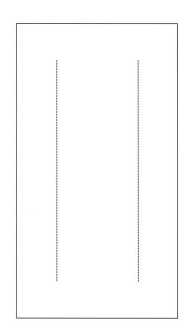

Ratio 9:4

0	9	27	72	90	117	144	162	216	324	360	450	540
0	4	12	32	40	52	64	72	96	144	160	200	240

WHICH RATIO DO YOU WANT?

Name: Date:

For each situation, look at each ratio and quickly decide which ratio you would choose. Then explain how you might convince others about your decision. Change your decision and argument if you find it is necessary.

1. You have just won a prize. You will be paid the money in five-dollar and one-dollar bills. You want the biggest prize you can get. Which ratio of five-dollar to one-dollar bills should you choose, 3:4 or 7:5? Justify your thinking.

2. You and a friend have been assigned to wash dishes after the school party. You do not like to wash dishes. Would you prefer to wash 7 dishes for every 11 your friend washes or 14 dishes for every 19 your friend washes? Justify your thinking.

3. Your gym teacher has assigned everyone to do sit-ups and jumping jacks but will let you decide how many sit-ups you do for each jumping jack. You prefer jumping jacks. Which ratio of sit-ups to jumping jacks will you choose, 5:6 or 11:12? Justify your thinking.

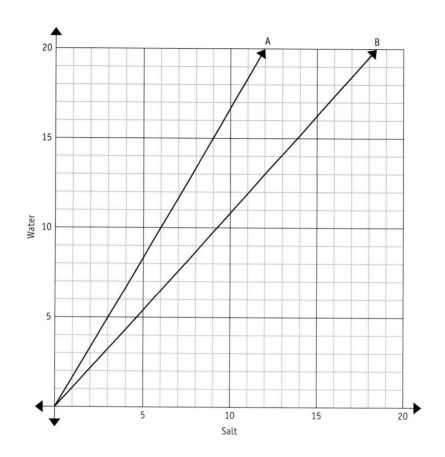

Copy the following cards onto card stock, cut them out, and laminate them if possible. Give each pair of students a complete set (blank boxes are included for you or your students to fill in with your own graphs or tables). To play, the two students arrange the cards facedown and take turns turning over two cards. If the cards match—that is, if the graph represents the data in the table—the player keeps the cards. If the cards do not match, the player turns them facedown and the opponent takes a turn. Play continues until students match all the cards.

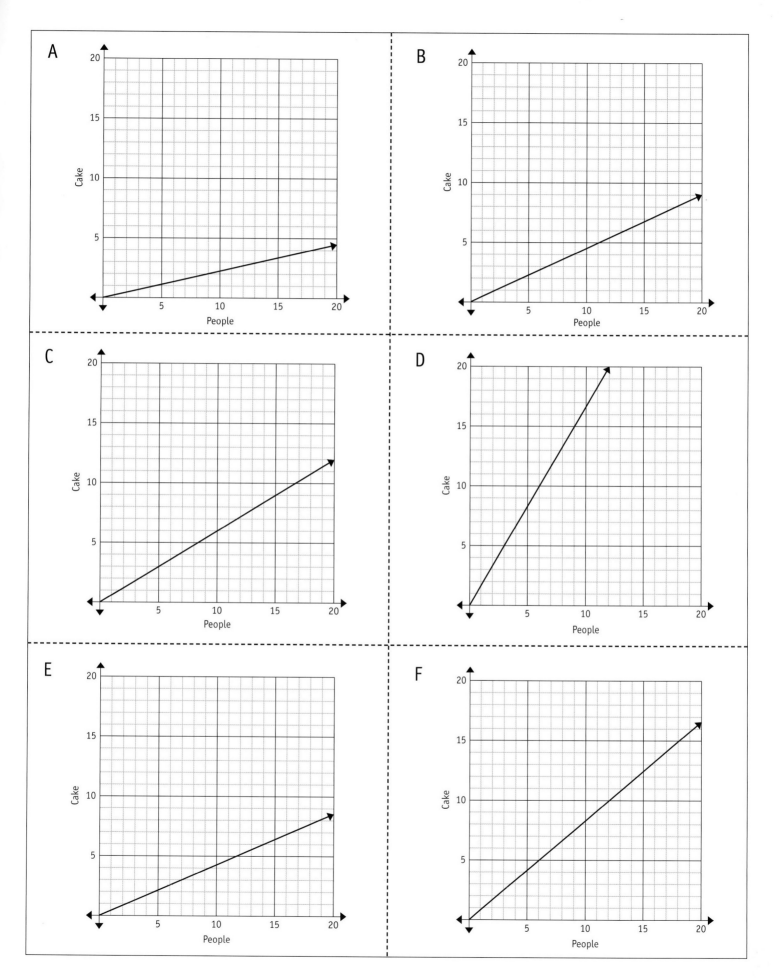

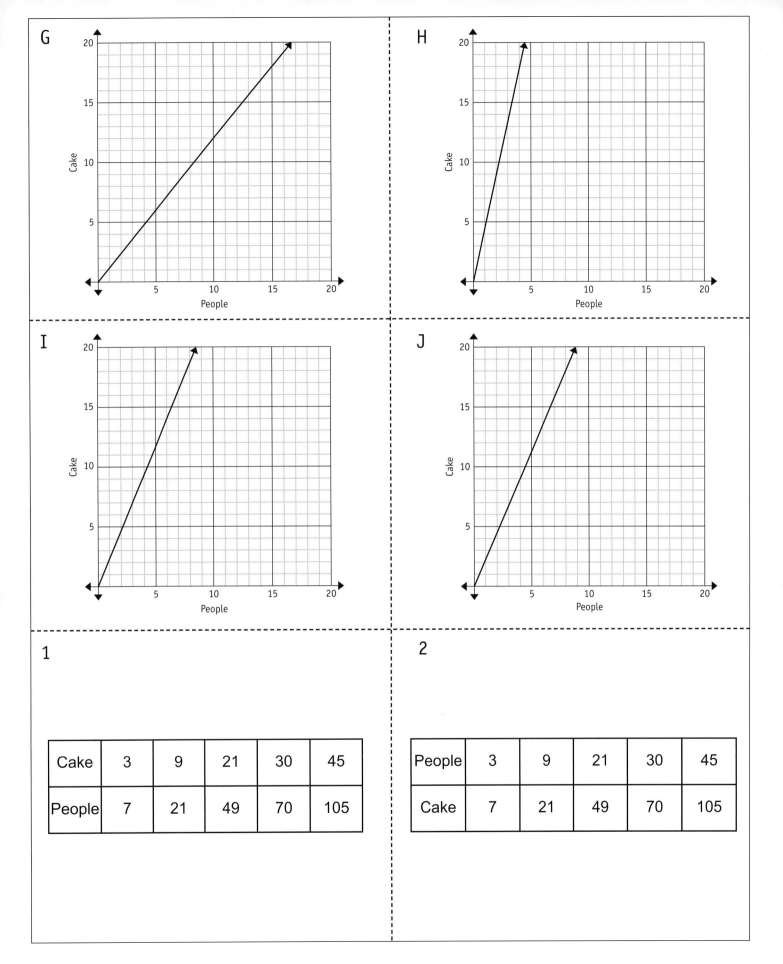

G

H

I

J

1

Cake	3	9	21	30	45
People	7	21	49	70	105

2

People	3	9	21	30	45
Cake	7	21	49	70	105

3

Cake	9	27	45	54	81
People	2	6	10	12	18

4

People	5	10	15	20	25
Cake	6	12	18	24	30

5

Cake	People
4	9
8	18
12	27
16	36
20	45

6

Cake	5	10	15	20	25
People	6	12	18	24	30

7

People	Cake
4	9
8	18
12	27
16	36
20	45

8

Cake	2	6	10	12	18
People	9	27	45	54	81

9

People	Cake
3	5
6	10
12	20
18	30
27	45

10

People	Cake
5	3
10	6
20	12
30	18
45	27

Name: Date:

1. Cole graphed the ratios of chocolate syrup to milk for three mixtures. For each mixture, what is the ratio of syrup to milk? Which mixture is the most chocolaty? Justify your answer.

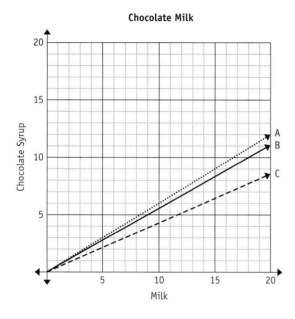

2. Chase has a collection of markers in the ratio of 5 red:7 blue. Mia has a collection in the ratio of 1 red:3 blue. Sophie has a ratio that is greater than Mia's but less than Chase's. What ratio of red to blue might Sophie have? Use the graph and justify your answer.

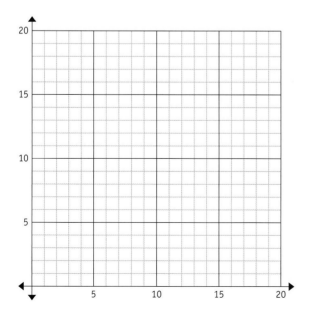

3. Pose a story problem that can be solved using a ratio table and a graph. Be sure to complete the representations and include a solution to your problem.

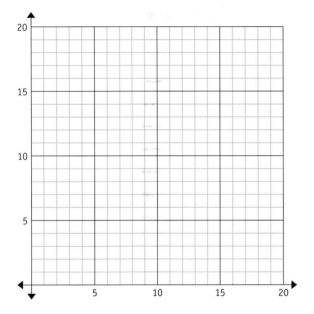

Name: Date:

Complete the decimal tables below by filling in an equivalent decimal value for each ratio.

Ratio	Decimal
8:8	
7:8	
6:8	
5:8	
4:8	
3:8	
2:8	
1:8	

Ratio	Decimal
10:10	
9:10	
8:10	
7:10	
6:10	
5:10	
4:10	
3:10	
2:10	
1:10	

Ratio	Decimal
6:6	
5:6	
4:6	
3:6	
2:6	
1:6	

Name: Date:

1. Record your data in the table.

Length of Radius	Circumference	How many times longer than the radius is the circumference?

2. What observations can you make about circles based upon the data in your table?

3. What ratio best represents the relationship between the circumference of a circle and the radius?

4. The Greek value for π is approximately 3.14 and the decimals continue on without repeating. How does this compare with your data? How does this relate to the formula for circumference?

MISSING DATA

Name: Date:

Complete the missing data, using your closest *estimates* when appropriate.

The radius of my circle is about _____ units in length because the circumference is about
                                      (1.)

100 units in length. When I know the circumference of a circle, I can use the following ratio
to find the radius: _____. If the radius of my circle is 20 units in length, then
                            (2.)

a close estimate of my circumference is _____ units in length. Sometimes when
                                                (3.)

I know the circumference of a circle, I am asked to estimate the diameter of that circle.
The ratio between the circumference of a circle and the diameter is _____. If
                                                                            (4.)

the circumference is 48 units, the diameter is about _____ units. If I divide the
                                                            (5.)

circumference by the diameter of a given circle, the solution will always be _____.
                                                                                    (6.)

The following equation is an efficient method for finding the circumference of a circle:
C = _____.
       (7.)

Name: Date:

For each of the following problems, you may use the representation of your choice to answer the questions, *but* you may not use the same representation for more than two problems.

1. During a recent student council election, Mario beat his opponent, Sam, by a ratio of 7:5 votes. If Mario received 91 votes, how many did Sam get? How many students voted?

2. Jayden was baby-sitting for two brothers, Juan and Dante. The number of building blocks that Juan had compared to the number Dante had was in the ratio of 3:4. If Juan gave $\frac{1}{2}$ of his blocks to his brother, what would the new ratio of Juan's blocks to Dante's be?

3. The ratio of girls to boys in the band was 9:8. Half of the boys left for soccer practice, which left 15 more girls than boys. How many students were in the band before the boys left? How many boys left for soccer practice?

4. **Challenge Problem:** If Sarah gave $2 to Tim, they would have an equal amount of money. But, if Tim gave $4 to Sarah, the ratio of Sarah's money to Tim's money would be 4:1. How much money did Sarah have in the beginning?

It's All Relative: Key Ideas and Common Misconceptions About Ratio and Proportion, Grades 6–7 by Anne Collins and Linda Dacey. Copyright © 2014. Stenhouse Publishers.

RATIOS AND UNIT RATES

Name: _____   Date: _____

Fill in each blank with an answer from the box below.

1. A ratio can be used to represent the _____ between two quantities.

2. A rate might represent _____ it takes to complete something.

3. Cassidy can address 24 envelopes in 8 minutes. This means that the ratio of envelopes to minutes is _____. The unit rate that represents how many envelopes Cassidy can address in 1 minute is _____ envelopes/minute.

4. Nicole has a collection of markers in the _____ of 6 red to 18 greens.

5. Carlos is paid $55.50 for working 6 hours at Dani's Deli. Carlos would be paid $37.00 for working _____ hours.

+--+
| **Answers** |
| |
| 3   difference   ratio   4   24:8 |
| |
| how long   relationship   rate   unit rate   proportion |
+--+

Identify the unit rate for each table.

6.

Ratio Table	
Red Paint	**Yellow Paint**
2 parts	3 parts
16 parts	24 parts

The unit rate is: _____

7.

Ratio Table	
Meters	**Time (sec.)**
25	3
75	9

The unit rate is: _____

Name: Date:

1. It takes 8 oz. of chocolate chips to make 1 batch of chocolate chip cookies. How many ounces of chocolate chips are needed to make 5 batches of these cookies for the bake sale?

2. The cook at the Good Morning Restaurant fried 120 eggs to make 40 orders of the breakfast special.

   a. What is the ratio of eggs to specials?

   b. What is the unit rate of eggs to specials?

   c. What is the ratio of specials to eggs?

   d. What is the unit rate of specials to eggs?

   e. Which unit rate would be most helpful when finding the number of specials you can make with 75 eggs? Justify your answer.

3. Mr. Chen used $3\frac{1}{2}$ cups of raisins to make 7 batches of oatmeal raisin cookies. How many cups of raisins would it take to make 1 batch of oatmeal raisin cookies? Justify your answer.

4. The food truck owner has $20 to buy pizza seasoning. With $1, she can buy $2\frac{1}{2}$ ounces of the seasoning. How many pounds of the seasoning can she buy? Justify your answer.

Name: Date:

In preparing for a weekend camping trip, you and your best friend have to go shopping for ground beef, corn, and hot dogs. Since you do not have a lot of money, you compare the advertisements from two grocery stores, Food for Less and Grocery Bargains.

Examine the following ads and determine which is the cheaper option for each food or if the options are equivalent. Show all your work and justify your answers.

Food for Less
Hamburger Patties
5lb. for $8.99

Grocery Bargains
Hamburger Patties
7lb for $10.99

Food for Less
Corn
8 ears for $11

Grocery Bargains
Corn
12 ears for $15

Food for Less
Hot Dogs
1lb. for $4.99, 1lb. free

Grocery Bargains
Hot Dogs
1lb. for $3.99

Name: Date:

Add two representations.

Table

Cans	Cost in $
1	1.17
3	**3.50**
6	7.00
9	10.50

Diagram

3 cans of corn at $3.50

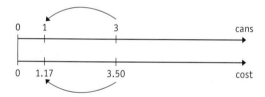

or $3.50 ÷ 3 = $1.17 per can

Graph

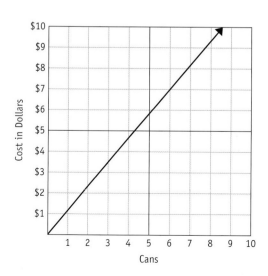

Table

Pounds	Cost in Dollars
1	0.75
3	2.75
6	5.50
12	**8.99 or 9.00**

Diagram

12 lb. of turkey at $8.99 (round up to $9.00)

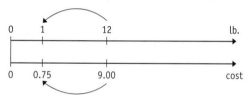

or $9.00 ÷ 12 lb. = $0.75 per lb.

$7\frac{1}{2}$ lb. bananas at $0.69 per lb.

$0.69 × $7\frac{1}{2}$ lb. = $5.18

Graph

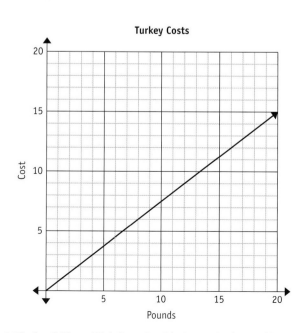

Name: Date:

1. A roll of shelf liner sells for $12. The roll is 12 in. $\times$ 20 ft.

    a. How many square inches are there in one roll?

    b. How much does one square inch of shelf paper cost?

2. Mr. Reynolds wants to carpet a bedroom that is 9 ft. by 12 ft. The carpet costs $22.50 per sq. yd. How much will the carpet for the room cost?

3. The following information is shown on a package of two large rolls of paper towels. Miguel wonders if the given total area is for the two rolls or for one roll. How can you convince him which it is?

Small sheets: 6″ $\times$ 11″
193 sheets per roll
Total area: 176.9 sq. ft.

4. Ms. Chen wants to tile the wall between the cabinets and the counter in the kitchen. The tiles are 1-inch squares and cost $12.99/sq. ft. She needs to fill a space that is 1.5 ft. by 6 ft. and another area above the sink that is 36 in. by 32 in. She wants to buy an extra 2 sq. ft. How much will she need to spend on all these tiles?

SCALING SCOTTIES

Name: Date:

1. Use two same-size elastic bands knotted together to make a "stretcher."

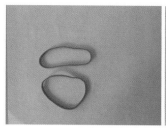 

2. If you are right-handed, tape a blank piece of paper to the right of the picture of the Scottie (or house) so the papers are touching. Tape down all corners so the papers do not shift.
3. If you are left-handed, tape a blank piece of paper to the left of the picture of the Scottie (or house) so the papers are touching. Tape down all corners so the papers do not shift.
4. Place one end of the elastic loop on the black dot to the side of the dog (or house) and place a sharpened pencil in the other end. Stretch the elastic until the knot, where you knotted the elastics together, is resting over the outline of the picture. Using the knot as your guide, trace the outline of the dog (or house) onto the blank piece of paper.
5. After completing your tracing, answer the following questions.
   a. What do you notice about the size of the dog (or house) you drew? How do the shapes of the original and the image compare?
   b. Use a ruler to measure various lengths of the original dog and the image of the dog. For example, the length of the tail, the length of the head, and the length of the dog between the front and rear paws. What do you notice? If you enlarged the house, measure the length of the house, the height of the house, the height of the door, and the length and width of the windows.
   c. Use an angle ruler and measure the angle formed at the dog's ears on both the original and the image. What do you notice about the measures of the angles? If you enlarged the house, what do you notice about the angle the roof makes at its peak as well as where it abuts the house?
   d. What scale factor best represents how the Scottie (or house) was enlarged?
   e. Cut out the original shape and use it to determine how many of the original shape might fit onto the image of the shape. About how many times greater is the area of the new figure than the original? How does this number relate to the scale factor?
   f. What do you think would happen to the various measurements if you used three elastics? Four elastics? *N* elastics? Why?
   g. Do you think it is possible to use a stretcher to get a smaller figure? A figure the same size? Try out your ideas to see if they work.

Right-Handed Scottie

Hold down your elastic here with your thumb.

Left-Handed Scottie

Hold down your elastic here with your thumb.

Right-Handed House

Hold down your elastic here with your thumb.

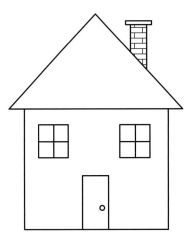

Left-Handed House

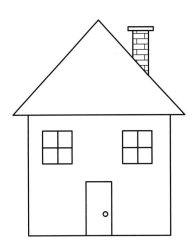

Hold down your elastic here with your thumb.

DOUBLE NUMBER LINES

Name: Date:

1. Given the following number lines and the problem situation, make a list of everything you can say about the relationship.

When I printed your homework problems, it took the copy machine 36 seconds to print 24 copies.

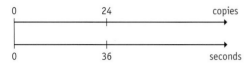

I noticed that:

_____
_____
_____
_____
_____
_____

2. Represent and solve the following.

When I printed your homework problems, it took the copy machine 36 seconds to print 24 copies. At this rate, how many copies can be made in 60 seconds?

Copy the following cards onto card stock, cut them out, and laminate them if possible. Distribute two lengths of rope or thick string to each pair of students. It works best if the students place their desks or tables side by side. Ask each student to record all of his or her work on a blank piece of paper or in their mathematics notebooks. Remind the students to include the three known values that they used to determine the missing value for each round of the game.

Directions:

1. Students place the cards facedown in a pile between them. They align the pieces of rope horizontally to form a double number line.

2. One student chooses a card and places it on one of the number lines.

3. The second student chooses a card and places it on the opposite number line, aligned with the first value to make the first ratio.

4. The first student then chooses a third card and places it on either of the lines, in a location relative to the other number already placed on that line.

   For example: The first card drawn is 15, the second card drawn is 6, and the third card drawn is 22.

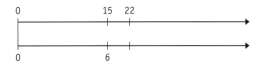

5. The students decide what labels to use for their number lines. For example, they may choose miles per hour, cost per pound, or words per minute.

6. Both students must now work to solve for the missing value. The first student to get the correct answer scores two points. (Students may use calculators to check their answers.) If a student gets an incorrect answer, he or she loses one point. The first person to earn twenty points wins.

7. Students discard the three cards on the number lines and draw another set of three cards.

1	3	9	24
32	16	7	25
65	4	8	12
50	6	5	1
14	22	10	36

Name: Date:

Use a graph and a double number line to solve the following problems. Justify your answers.

If a snail travels 3 inches in 8 minutes, how far will it travel in 1 minute? How far will this snail travel in 15 minutes if the snail continues at the same rate of speed?

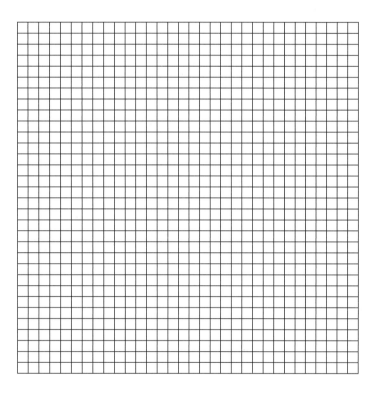

HOW FAR MIGHT THEY TRAVEL?

Name: _____   Date: _____

Many large animals move at rapid rates of speed. The following are the average rates of speed for three large cats.

Cheetah

17.75 miles in 15 minutes

Lion

52,800 feet in 12 minutes

Jaguar

96,703.2 feet in 20 minutes

Answer the following questions, assuming that the animals travel at a constant rate of speed. Justify your answers.

1. How many feet are in 1 mile? _____ feet/mile

2. How far can a cheetah travel in 1 hour? _____ miles

3. How far can a lion travel in $\frac{1}{2}$ hour? _____ miles

4. How far can a jaguar travel in 1.5 hours? _____ miles

5. How long will it take a cheetah to travel 63 miles? _____

6. How long will it take a lion to travel $3\frac{1}{2}$ miles? _____

7. How long will it take a jaguar to travel 10 miles? _____

8. Which animal moves more quickly than the others? _____

It's All Relative: Key Ideas and Common Misconceptions About Ratio and Proportion, Grades 6–7 by Anne Collins and Linda Dacey. Copyright © 2014. Stenhouse Publishers.

GIANT AND TINY CHAIRS

Name: Date:

Emma sat on three different-size chairs (see pictures). The seat of each chair is a square. Following are Emma's measurements:

- From the seat to the top of her head: 54 cm
- From her back to the top of her boots: 47.5 cm
- The height of her boots: 17 cm
- The length of her back to her knee: 25 cm
- The length of the smallest seat is $\frac{1}{4}$ the length of the largest seat.
- The smallest seat measures 9 inches on each side.

1. Based upon her sit measurements, determine the approximate heights of each chair and the dimensions of each seat.

2. If we stacked the smallest chairs one on top of another, how many chairs would we need to stack to reach the same height as the largest chair?

3. How many of the smallest seats would fit onto the largest seat?

4. What scale factor was applied to the normal-size chair to get the height of the smallest chair?

5. What scale factor was applied to the normal-size chair to get the height of the largest chair?

6. If you applied a scale factor of $\frac{5}{2}$ to the normal-size chair, what would the new height be?

7. If you applied a scale factor of 8 to the smallest chair, what would the dimensions of the new seat be?

It's All Relative: Key Ideas and Common Misconceptions About Ratio and Proportion, Grades 6–7 by Anne Collins and Linda Dacey. Copyright © 2014. Stenhouse Publishers.

Name: Date:

1. Which of the following rectangles are proportional to one another? How do you know?

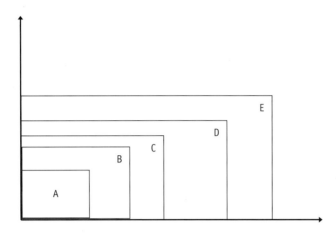

2. Are the values in these tables proportional? Justify your response.

Table 1

Input	Output
3	7
12	28
15	35
21	49

Table 2

Input	Output
7	21
15	30
23	39
30	60

It's All Relative: Key Ideas and Common Misconceptions About Ratio and Proportion, Grades 6–7 by Anne Collins and Linda Dacey. Copyright © 2014. Stenhouse Publishers.

Name: Date:

1. Which of the following tables shows a proportional growth? Justify your reasoning.

Table A

5	3
20	15
35	18
65	39

Table B

3	8
27	72
15	40
18	48

2. Read each of the following story situations and determine whether or not it represents a proportional relationship. If not, *change the ratio values so they are proportional.*

   a. Noah and Jacob want to paint together. They each want to use exactly the same color. Noah uses 3 cans of yellow paint and 6 cans of red paint. Jacob uses 7 cans of yellow paint and 21 cans of red paint. Are the boys using the same paint mixture? Justify your thinking.

   b. A printing press takes exactly 12 minutes to print 14 dictionaries. It can print $25\frac{5}{7}$ dictionaries in 30 minutes. Is this a proportional relationship? Justify your thinking.

3. Which of the following figures are proportional? Justify your answer. Draw a figure that is proportional to Figure A and one that is proportional to Figure C.

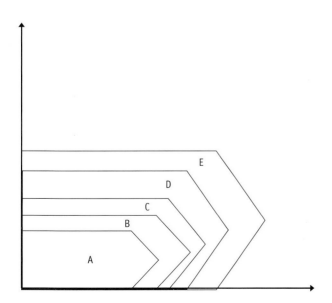

HUMAN PROPORTIONS

Name: _____   Date: _____

Work with a partner to measure the following:

- the length of your thumb
- the length of your hand from your wrist to the tip of your middle finger
- the length of your forearm from your elbow to your wrist
- the length of your foot in inches
- your arm span from the tip of the middle finger of your right hand across your back to the tip of the middle finger of your left hand
- your height

1. Write a ratio comparing each of the following measurements.

   a. the length of your thumb to the length of your hand _____
   b. the length of your forearm to the length of your foot _____
   c. your arm span to your height _____

2. Complete the following table using your ratio data and that of three other students.

Measure	Student A	Student B	Student C	Student D	Average Ratio
thumb:hand					
forearm:foot					
arm span:height					

3. Use the data from your table to find the missing values comparing the measures of a 6-foot human to a giant who measures about 72 feet tall.

Measure	Human (inches)	Giant (feet)
thumb	2.7 in.	
hand		9.36 ft.
forearm		10.4 ft.
foot		
arm span		
height	72 in.	

Name: Date:

1. Yolanda and her family were taking a trip from Norwood, Massachusetts, to Montreal, Quebec, Canada. As they started their trip, she noticed a sign on the highway that said the distance from Norwood to Dedham, Massachusetts, was 4 miles or 6.4 kilometers. Her dad told her the distance from Norwood to Montreal was about 523 kilometers. How many miles are between Norwood and Montreal? How long will it take to drive from Norwood to Montreal if the family averages 65 miles per hour and does not stop between those two locations?

2. Courtney converted some US money into Canadian dollars. She received $163.20 in exchange for her US money and was told the exchange rate was $1.02 Canadian dollars to the US dollar (so for every $1.00 US, she got $1.02 CD). How much US money did she convert?

3. You are helping to keep a journal of the vacation expenses. You record the number of miles traveled and the amount of gas the car takes at each gas station. How many miles per gallon did the car get if you traveled 358 miles on 14 gallons of gas? At this rate, how far could you go on 150 gallons of gas?

VACATION TRAVELS

Name: _____   Date: _____

Fill in the blanks using the data from the box below. Circle the strategy you used to find each solution: either SF for scale factor or UR for unit rate.

Our car gets 27.5 miles per gallon. On the first leg of our trip, we used 42 gallons of gas and traveled (1.) _____ miles. (SF or UR) We stopped for a picnic lunch and paid $5.29 for 3 pounds of hot dogs, which cost (2.) $_____ per pound. (SF or UR)

    When we got back on the road, the legend on the map indicated that 3 inches were equivalent to 246 miles. The distance on the map between our rest stop and Sault Ste. Marie, Michigan, was $6\frac{1}{2}$ inches, or (3.) _____ miles. (SF or UR) When we stopped to make camp, my sister and I went for a bicycle ride. Because it stayed light so late, we were able to ride for 2 hours and travel 24 kilometers. At this speed, it would take us (4.) _____ hours to bicycle the 144 kilometers to Mackinac Island. (SF or UR)

    In the morning our family decided to drive across the border to Canada. When I looked at the speedometer, I noticed the car was traveling at just under 90 km/hr., or just over (5.) _____ mi./hr. (SF or UR) We stopped to buy penny candy, which was being sold for $2.49 CD per $\frac{1}{4}$ lb., or (6.) $_____ CD per pound. (SF or UR) Among all of us, we spent a whopping $35.64 Canadian, which was (7.) $_____ US (SF or UR) for (8.) _____ lb. of candy. (SF or UR) My parents were blown away that the candy cost so much money!

    In all, we traveled 6,400 miles, or (9.) _____ kilometers this summer. (SF or UR) We spent an average of $3.52 US per gallon for gas, for a total of approximately (10.) $_____ US (SF or UR) or (11.) $_____ CD. (SF or UR)

835.58	1.77	232.73	3.50	1,155	9.96
12	10,300	533	55	34.94	819.20

I find it is easier for me to use scale factors to solve proportional problems when:

_____

I find it is easier for me to use unit rates to solve proportional problems when:

_____

It's All Relative: Key Ideas and Common Misconceptions About Ratio and Proportion, Grades 6–7 by Anne Collins and Linda Dacey. Copyright © 2014. Stenhouse Publishers.   **A42**

PROBLEM STARTERS

Copy the following cards onto card stock and cut them out. Create five work areas in your classroom and place one card at each area.

Here's the representation. What is the problem?

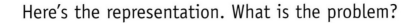

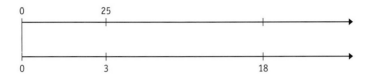

Here's the answer. What is the problem?

The unit rate is 3 times at bat/hit.

Here's the data. What's the problem?

3 tennis balls per can
72 balls per case
456 tennis balls
$65.99 per case

Here's the equation. What's the problem?

$$\frac{25}{t} = \frac{75}{96}$$

Here's the context. What's the problem?

Downloading songs or movies.

Name: Date:

Write story problems that can be modeled by the following proportions or situations.

1. $\frac{23}{n} = \frac{92}{237}$

2. The scale factor is $\frac{3}{5}$

3.

4	6
12	18
24	36
44	66

4.

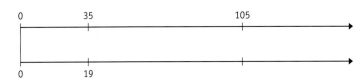

Name: Date:

Shade in the following grids to illustrate the percent value for the given ratios.

1. 1:4

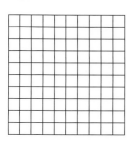

1:4 = _____%

2. 1:5

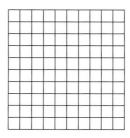

1:5 = _____%

3. 3:4

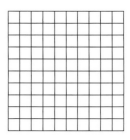

3:4 = _____%

4. 1:6

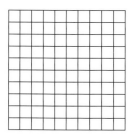

1:6 = _____%

5. 5:8

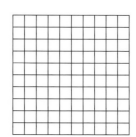

5:8 = _____%

6. 2:3

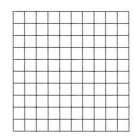

2:3 = _____%

7. 1:3

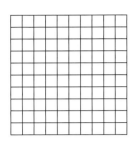

1:3 = _____%

8. 5:6

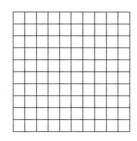

5:6 = _____%

9. 4:9

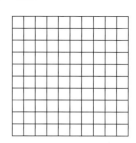

4:9 = _____%

Name: Date:

Value	Percent

Value	Percent

Value	Percent

Value	Percent

Copy the following cards onto card stock, cut them out, and laminate them if possible. Give one set of cards to each pair of students. Pairs should shuffle the cards and work together to sort and match the cards that have equivalent values.

A	7
45% of $160	$80 − $8 = $72

2	B
$32.00 + $6.40 = $38.40	$12\frac{1}{2}$% of $160

C	D
24% of $160	8% of $160

8	E
$160.00 − $32.00 + $4.80 = $132.80	16% of $160

3	F
$\$160 \div 8 = \$20$	83% of $160

G	4
120% of $160	$\$160 + \$16 + \$16 = \$192$

9	6
$\$16.00 + \$9.60 = \$25.60$	$\$16.00 - \$3.20 = \$12.80$

H	5
135% of $160	$\$160 + \$16 + \$40 = \$216$

I	1
185% of $160	$\$160 + \$16 + \$120 = \$296$

Directions:

1. Place the student desks or tables in lines *with not more than 5 students per line.*

2. Provide the last student in each line with a small whiteboard, a dry-erase marker, and an eraser.

3. Choose one of the problems on the next page and project it on the board.

4. Direct all students to solve the problem, and tell the student in each line with the whiteboard to record his or her work on the whiteboard.

5. When that student is finished, he or she should pass the whiteboard, marker, and eraser forward to the person sitting in front of him or her. The next student either agrees with the solution and passes the materials forward *or* makes any necessary corrections and then passes the materials forward. This process repeats itself until each student in the line has had a chance to examine, revise, and agree with the solution.

6. After receiving and reviewing the whiteboard, the person in the front of the line holds the board up for you to see. If it is correct, give a thumbs-up. If it is incorrect, give a thumbs-down.

   - If the team's work is correct, the first person in the line takes the whiteboard, marker, and eraser and moves to the back of the line, and all of the other students move forward one seat.

   - If the team's work is incorrect, the first person in the line passes the whiteboard, marker, and eraser back to the last person in the line.

7. Project the next problem for the students to solve.

8. The first team to have students rotate back to their original seats wins the round.

1. The following rectangle represents $\frac{3}{4}$ of the whole figure. How might the whole look? ┌─────────────────────┐ │ │ └─────────────────────┘	2. Sixty percent of the soccer league's budget is $9,000. What is the soccer league's budget?
3. Chandra has saved $350, or 70% of what she needs to buy the dirt bike she wants. How much does the dirt bike cost?	4. At the end of the school year, a store gave away 40% off coupons for team jerseys. Niki bought a jersey for $12. What was the original price of the jersey?
5. Thirteen members, or about 37%, of the cheerleading squad were invited to participate in the regional finals. How many cheerleaders are there?	6. Forty-two percent, or 84, of the blood donors at a blood drive had O-positive blood. How many people donated blood?
7. Manuel bought a sweater for $36. He paid 75% of the original price. What was the original cost of the sweater?	8. Henry answered 76 questions on his test correctly. He answered only 5% of the questions incorrectly. How many questions were on his test?
9. There are 18 girls in Amy's class, which is 56.25% of the class. How many students are there in Amy's class?	10. Sierra has 72% of the mosaic tiles she needs for her art project. This translates into 540 tiles. How many tiles does she need in all?
11. At college, Korinda spends $230 on food each month, which is 23% of what she earns. How much does Korinda earn each month?	12. Kevin bought a hoodie for 76% of its original price. He paid $28.50. What was the original price of the hoodie?

MATCH IT AND PROVE IT

Copy the following problems and answers onto card stock and cut them out. Working in pairs, students shuffle the question cards and spread them faceup on their tables or desks. Next, they shuffle the answer cards and place them facedown in a pile. The first student turns over an answer card, and both students compete to match a problem to the correct answer, and prove that the match is mathematically correct. The person who matches the question and answer correctly keeps both cards. If neither student gets the correct answer, the answer card is placed at the bottom of the answer card pile. Students take turns turning over the answer card. (*Note:* These cards can also be used in *Play It Forward*, as there are multiple question types included in this set.)

Questions

A	B	C
A tip of 15% for a bill of $45.	A 6% tax on a video game that costs $19.99.	The cost of a $15 book after a 7% sales tax.
D	**E**	**F**
A 20% tip for a meal that cost $32.	School supplies cost $72. A tax of 5% is added to the subtotal. What is the total bill?	Jackson pays $156 for his sports equipment. The tax is 5%. What is the final cost?
G	**H**	**I**
Isabelle gave a $4.50 tip for a meal that cost $30.00. What percent tip did she give?	The sales tax is 4.5%. If you buy a bicycle that costs $150, how much will you pay?	The sales tax in one state is 4.5%. How much tax will you pay on a skate board that costs $78?
J	**K**	**L**
Mrs. Gates left a $16 tip for a meal that cost $80. What percent tip did she leave?	If you paid $50, including tip, for a meal that cost $42, what percent tip did you leave?	Josie bought a friend a birthday present that cost $38 plus 5% tax. How much money did she spend?

M	N	O
Matthew paid $84 on a bill that came to $63. What percent tip did he leave?	Julia's mom sells real estate. She sold a house for $189,000 and received a 3% commission. How much money did she earn in commission?	Noah has a paper route and receives a 2% commission on the papers he sells. If he sells $145 worth of papers, what will his commission be?

Answers

$6.75	$1.20	$16.05
$6.40	$75.60	$163.80
15%	$156.75	$3.51
20%	19%	$39.90
$33\frac{1}{3}$%	$5,670	$2.90

INCREASE PROBLEMS

1. Liam collects miniature trains. He realizes that since he bought his last train, the price has increased by 45%. If he paid $55 for his last train, what will the new train cost? Justify your answer.

2. For three years, Jesse saved all his money to buy a fancy racing bike. He priced the bike he wanted when he began saving, but when he went to the store to buy it, he saw the price had increased by 20%. The bike now cost $768. How much did the bike originally cost? Justify your answer.

3. Aleeyah's grandmother gave her some Games Forever stock for her birthday. In one year the value of the stock rose from $38 per share to $43.70. By what percent did the stock rise? Justify your answer.

4. The world population in 1950 was 2.6 billion. In 2009, it reached 6.8 billion. By what percent had the world population grown? Justify your answer.

5. The world population in 2009 was 6.8 billion. It is estimated that in 2043 the population will have grown to 9 billion. By what percent will the world population grow if this estimate is accurate? Justify your answer.

PERCENT STORIES

Name: _____   Date: _____

Use some of the values in the box to complete each story. The story must make sense.

1. Tim and his brother play basketball 4 days a week, which is about _____% of the days per week. Tim usually makes 70% of the shots he attempts. If he takes 36 shots, he expects to make _____ baskets. One night Tim made 47 of the 65 attempts he took, for a _____% shooting rate. When he plays basketball for his team, he usually scores on 4 of every 9 attempts, for a _____% shooting rate. He much prefers playing with his brother.

72	25	
	65	
	44	57
28		

2. Noah collects comic books. Last month he saw a first edition comic book for $65. This month he saw the price had increased 15%, or $_____. He paid $_____ for it because he was afraid the price would keep going up. Noah said he would sell it for $_____, or a _____% profit. Noah's dad told him to keep the comic book for a longer period of time or until he could get $100, or a _____% increase on his initial investment.

74.75		34
	80	
20		
	7.48	
9.75	7	

3. Sophia works with her family at local flea markets. She bakes and sells cookies. She sold a dozen cookies for $3.50, but her mom told her to raise the price 6%. This would add _____ cents to the price. If she does as her mom says, the new price of the cookies will be $_____. Her dad thinks she should sell the cookies for $6.00 a dozen, which would be about a _____% increase. Sophia compromises and sells the cookies for $_____ a dozen, which is about a _____% increase. She makes $_____ when she sells _____ dozen at this price.

5	21	
	10	71
43	3.71	
	2.75	50

It's All Relative: Key Ideas and Common Misconceptions About Ratio and Proportion, Grades 6–7 by Anne Collins and Linda Dacey. Copyright © 2014. Stenhouse Publishers.

PERCENT MATH-O

Directions:

1. Make a copy of the Math-O card (see next page) for each student.
2. Pass out a blank card to each student together with a handful of plastic discs or other tokens.
3. Instruct the students to choose twenty-four of the values on the reproducible and randomly place them on their Math-O cards.
4. Instruct students to place a disc on the Math-O space.
5. To play a whole-class game, call out problems in random order (see page A58). Students place their discs on equivalent values. The first student to get five discs in a row calls out "Math-O!" and wins the round.
6. To play the game in small groups, make one copy of the problems per group on card stock. Cut out the problems and laminate them if possible. Students shuffle the problem cards, and one student in the group turns the cards over one at a time, reading each problem aloud. Students place their discs on equivalent values. The first student to get five discs in a row calls out "Math-O!" and wins the round.

Encourage students to compute mentally!

Math-O Card Values

5%	50%	10%	15%	20%	30%
40%	60%	70%	80%	90%	100%
200%	150%	0.5%	$66\frac{2}{3}\%$	$83\frac{1}{3}\%$	175%
$11\frac{1}{9}\%$	$12\frac{1}{2}\%$	$62\frac{1}{2}\%$	75%	$87\frac{1}{2}\%$	$22\frac{2}{9}\%$
$44\frac{4}{9}\%$	$55\frac{5}{9}\%$	$77\frac{7}{9}\%$	$88\frac{8}{9}\%$	125%	130%
140%	160%	170%	180%	1%	95%

Math-O-Card

		MATH-O Free space		

Math-O Problems

Call out the following problems in random order. It is helpful to place a check beside each one you use. You may also use the Math-O card to practice ratio-to-percent conversions for a quick skills practice.

1. An increase from $80 to $160	100%
2. A decrease from $90 to $20	$77\frac{7}{9}$%
3. A decrease from $70 to $35	50%
4. A decrease from $120 to $108	10%
5. A decrease from $300 to $15	95%
6. A decrease from $180 to $160	$11\frac{1}{9}$%
7. A decrease from $500 to $200	60%
8. An increase from $16 to $48	200%
9. An increase from $25 to $30	20%
10. An increase from $200 to $225	$12\frac{1}{2}$%
11. An increase from $40 to $46	15%
12. An increase from $27 to $33	$22\frac{2}{9}$%
13. An increase from $400 to $420	5%
14. An increase from $60 to $84	40%
15. An increase from $400 to $750	$87\frac{1}{2}$%
16. An increase from $90 to $252	180%
17. A decrease from $900 to $300	$66\frac{2}{3}$%
18. A decrease from $700 to $210	70%
19. A decrease from $360 to $60	$83\frac{1}{3}$%
20. A decrease from $20 to $2	90%
21. A decrease from $50 to $49.75	0.5%
22. A decrease from $64 to $24	$62\frac{1}{2}$%
23. A decrease from $360 to $200	$44\frac{4}{9}$%
24. A decrease from $750 to $525	30%
25. A decrease from $100 to $99	1%
26. A decrease from $25 to $5	80%
27. A decrease from $54 to $6	$88\frac{8}{9}$%
28. A decrease from $63 to $28	$55\frac{5}{9}$%
29. An increase from $20 to $54	170%
30. An increase from $80 to $140	75%
31. An increase from $2 to $5	150%
32. An increase from $1,000 to $2,250	125%
33. An increase from $10 to $23	130%
34. An increase from $25 to $60	140%
35. An increase from $40 to $104	160%
36. An increase from $160 to $440	175%

It's All Relative: Key Ideas and Common Misconceptions About Ratio and Proportion, Grades 6–7 by Anne Collins and Linda Dacey. Copyright © 2014. Stenhouse Publishers.

Name: _____   Date: _____

Write a word problem that includes the given words and numbers. You may include other numbers as well. Then solve the problem.

1. | 275   prefer swimming   45% |

2. | 27%   miles per hour   42%   45 |

3. | percent decrease   12%   profit per sale $452.25 |

SOLVING PROBLEMS

Name: _____   Date: _____

Solve the following problems. Use a diagram, table, or graph to support your solution.

1. The Aspell Middle School athletic director buys 20% more baseballs each year than he does softballs. This year he bought 176 balls. How many baseballs and how many softballs did he purchase?

2. The Sullivan Middle School purchased new mathematics books for grade six and grade seven. The principal ordered 35% more grade six books than grade seven books. If he bought a total of 470 mathematics books, how many were for grade six and how many were for grade seven?

3. Katie makes bows for patriotic holidays. She orders red and blue ribbon in the ratio of 7 yards to 5 yards. If she bought a total of 636 yards, what percentage of the ribbon was red?

4. The Quincy Scholarship Fund sold tickets to its annual town barbecue. Last year, the group sold a total of 1,530 tickets in the ratio of 4 adult tickets for every 5 child tickets. This year, the group sold 20% more child tickets. How many child tickets did the group sell this year?

It's All Relative: Key Ideas and Common Misconceptions About Ratio and Proportion, Grades 6–7 by Anne Collins and Linda Dacey. Copyright © 2014. Stenhouse Publishers.

What's My Ratio? Recording Sheet

Answers will vary.

Script

No answer.

Planning Your Script

Answers will vary.

Equivalent Ratios

1. a.

Color A	2	4	10	24	30	160	180	200
Color B	7	14	35	84	105	560	630	700

b. Answers will vary.

2.

Hits	3	9	21	39	57	81	90	117
At Bats	4	12	28	52	76	108	120	156

3. Possible answers include 3:8; 6:16; 9:24; 12:32; and 15:40.

How Might Ratios Look?

1.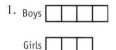

2. There were 32 boys and 24 girls.

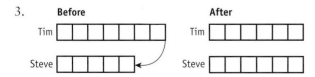

56 ÷ 7 cells = 8. Each cell = 8, so there are 8 × 4 boys and 8 × 3 girls.

3.

Before   **After**

Tim □□□□□□□   Tim □□□□□□

Steve □□□□□   Steve □□□□□□

Each cell represents a change of 12, so Tim had 84 cards in the beginning.

4. Gina scored 56 points, Belle scored 80 points, and Katie scored 96 points.

□□□□□□□□□□□□□□□□□□□□□□□□□□□□□ = 232

232 ÷ 29 = 8, so each cell represents 8. 8 × 7 = 56, 8 × 10 = 80, and 8 × 12 = 96.

Double Up

Note that the equivalent ratio is identified in lowest terms, but any of the ratios chosen from the preceding list would be correct.

1. 6:1; 18:3; 24:4; 30:5; 36:6; answers will vary for the last set of tick marks. All ratios are equivalent to 6:1.

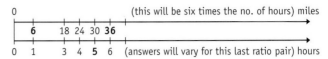

2. 2.5:1; 10:4; 20:8; answers may vary (25:10; 35:14; etc.); 40:16; 80:32. All ratios are equivalent to 5:2.

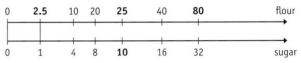

3. 1:$3.50; 18:$63.00; 27:$94.50; 54:$189.00; 63:$220.50; 81:$283.50. All ratios are equivalent to 1:$3.50.

0	1	18	27	54	63	**81**	books

| 0 | **3.50** | 63.00 | 94.50 | **189.00** | **220.50** | 283.50 | cost ($) |

Ratio Slide Rules

No answer.

Which Ratio Do You Want?

1. 7:5. The ratio of 3:4 yields $15 for every $4, while the ratio of 7:5 yields $35 for every $5.
2. 7:11. If you compare the number of dishes you wash to the number your friend washes in a table, you can see that when you wash 14 dishes, your friend washes 22. This is a better deal than you having to wash 14 dishes for your friend's 19 dishes.
3. 5:6. An equivalent ratio to 5:6 is 10:12; this means that for every 12 jumping jacks you have to do 10 sit-ups—not 11 sit-ups as you would have to do with the ratio of 11:12.

Which Is Saltier?

Line A is saltier because it is closest to the axis labeled "Salt" (or, the greater the amount of water, the less salty).

Match It

Graph	Table	Ratio of Cake to People
A	8	2:9
B	5	4:9
C	10	3:5
D	9	5:3
E	1	3:7
F	6	5:6
G	4	6:5
H	3	9:2
I	2	7:3
J	7	9:4

Graph It

1. Line A: (11,5); Line B (7,4); Line C: (10,7). Line A is the most chocolaty.
2. Any ratio between $\frac{7}{21}$ and $\frac{15}{21}$ is acceptable, including 1:2; 3:5; 3:7; and 4:7.

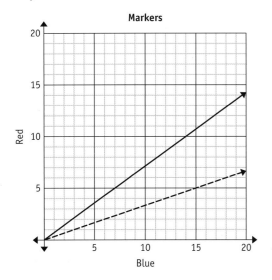

3. Answers will vary.

Conversion Tables

1.

Ratio	Decimal
8:8	1.000
7:8	0.875
6:8	0.750
5:8	0.625
4:8	0.500
3:8	0.375
2:8	0.250
1:8	0.125

2.

Ratio	Decimal
10:10	1.0
9:10	0.9
8:10	0.8
7:10	0.7
6:10	0.6
5:10	0.5
4:10	0.4
3:10	0.3
2:10	0.2
1:10	0.1

3.

Ratio	Decimal
6:6	1.00
5:6	0.8$\overline{3}$
4:6	0.6$\overline{6}$
3:6	0.50
2:6	0.3$\overline{3}$
1:6	0.1$\overline{6}$

Pi Recording Sheet

1. Answers will vary. For example:
   - radius 1, circumference 6.28, about 6 times greater
   - radius 10, circumference 62.8, about 6 times greater
   - radius 5, circumference 31.4, about 6 times greater
2. No matter how large or small the radius, the circumference is 6 times greater.
3. $C = 2\pi r$ or $C/2r = \pi$

Missing Data

1. 16 or 17 (Answers may vary, as this is an estimate.)
2. 6:1 or $r = \frac{C}{2\pi}$
3. 120 (Answers may vary, as this is an estimate.)
4. 3:1 or $\frac{C}{d} = \pi$
5. 15 or 16 (Answers may vary, as this is an estimate.)
6. π
7. πd or $2\pi r$

Choose Your Own Method

1. Sam received 65 votes. One hundred fifty-six students voted.
2. The new ratio would be 3:11.
3. There were 51 students in the band. Twelve boys left for soccer.
4. Sarah had $12.

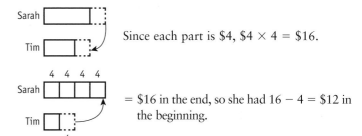

Since each part is $4, $4 × 4 = $16.

= $16 in the end, so she had 16 − 4 = $12 in the beginning.

Ratios and Unit Rates

1. relationship
2. how long
3. 24:8; 3
4. ratio
5. 4
6. $\frac{2}{3}$ part red paint per 1 part yellow paint
7. $8\frac{1}{3}$ meters per second

Cooking

1. 40 ounces
2. a. 120 eggs:40 breakfast specials or a ratio of 3:1
   b. 3 eggs per breakfast special
   c. 40 breakfast specials:120 eggs or a ratio of 1:3
   d. $\frac{1}{3}$ breakfast special per egg
   e. Answers will vary; many students will prefer 3 eggs per breakfast special.
3. $\frac{1}{2}$ cup
4. $3\frac{1}{8}$ lbs. or 3.125 lbs.

Camping Out

Note: You may want to observe whether any students round up to the nearest penny to work with whole numbers using their estimation skills.

Hamburger Patties: Grocery Bargains is a better deal with a unit price of $1.57 per pound, while Food for Less has a unit rate of $1.80 per pound.

Ears of Corn: Grocery Bargains is a better deal with a unit price of $1.25 per ear, while Food for Less has a unit rate of $1.38 per ear.

Hot Dogs: It depends on how many pounds of hot dogs the friends buy. If they want to buy 1 pound, Grocery Bargains is a better deal with a unit price of $3.99 per pound. If they want to buy more than 1 pound, Food for Less is a better deal with a unit price of $2.50 per pound.

Possible Representations

No answer.

Covering Spaces

1. a. 2,880 square inches
   b. $0.004 per square inch of shelf paper, which would round up to $0.01
2. $270
3. For two rolls, a possible explanation would be that one sheet is 66 squares inches, so one roll is 193 sheets × 66 square inches, or 12,738 square inches. If you divide 12,738 square inches by 144 square inches (the number of square inches per square foot), it's about 88 square feet, and that is about half of the stated square feet.
4. $246.81

Scaling Scotties

5. a. Answers will vary.
   b. Answers will vary.
   c. Answers will vary.
   d. Answers will vary.
   e. Answers will vary, but they should be the square of the scale factor.
   f. Answers will vary.
   g. Answers will vary.

Scaling Houses

No answer.

Double Number Lines

1. Answers will vary.
2. 40 copies

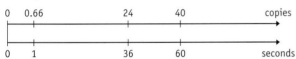

Find My Matching Value

No answer.

Snail on the Move

The snail will travel $\frac{3}{8}$ inches in 1 minute and $5\frac{5}{8}$ inches in 15 minutes.

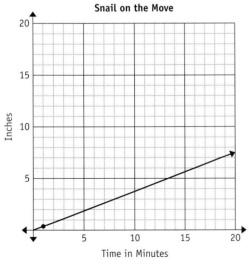

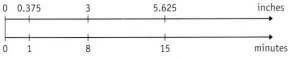

How Far Might They Travel?

1. 5,280
2. 71
3. 25
4. 82.4175 (or an appropriate rounded number)
5. 53.24 minutes (or an appropriate rounded number)
6. 4.2 minutes
7. 10.92 minutes
8. The cheetah is the fastest. One justification is unit rates: the cheetah travels at 6,248 feet per minute, the lion travels at 4,400 feet per minute, and the jaguar travels at 4,835.16 feet per minute.

Giant and Tiny Chairs

Answers are approximate, and reasonable answers should be accepted.

1. The largest chair is 72 inches or 182.88 cm tall; the normal-size chair is 36 inches or 91.44 cm tall; and the smallest chair is 18 inches or 45.72 cm tall.
2. 4 small chairs
3. 16 small seats
4. 1:2
5. 2:1
6. 90 inches or 228.6 cm
7. 72 inches by 72 inches or 182.88 cm by 182.88 cm

Class Starter for Am I Proportional?

1. A and B are proportional. D and E are proportional.
2. Table 1 is proportional. Table 2 is not proportional.

Am I Proportional?

1. Table A is not proportional. Table B is proportional.
2. a. The boys are not using the same paint mixture. One justification is that Steve's mixture has a unit rate of 1:2 and Jacob's has a unit rate of 1:3. Answers will vary on how to make the relationship proportional, but one example is that Jacob should use 7 cans of yellow paint and 14 cans of red.
   b. This is not a proportional relationship because the scale factor between 12 minutes and 14 dictionaries is 2.5 but the scale factor between 30 minutes and $25\frac{5}{7}$ dictionaries is about 1.17.
3. A and B are proportional; D and E are proportional. Students may draw a diagonal from the origin through the opposite vertex. If the line goes through both vertices, the figures are proportional.

Human Proportions

1–2. Students' measurements will vary. Compare average ratios from each group.

3.

Measure	Human (inches)	Giant (feet)
thumb	2.7 in.	2.7 ft.
hand	9.36 in.	9.36 ft.
forearm	10.4 in.	10.4 ft.
foot	10.4 in.	10.4 ft.
arm span	72 in.	72 ft.
height	72 in.	72 ft.

Class Starter for Vacation Travels
1. There are about 325 miles between Norwood and Montreal. It will take 5 hours to drive that distance if they do not stop.
2. $160
3. The car got 25.57 mpg. You could go 3,835.7 miles.
4. 57 liters. 1 gal = 3.8 liters, so 15 gal × 3.8 liters/gal = 57 liters.

Vacation Travels
1. 1,155
2. 1.77
3. 533
4. 12
5. 55
6. 9.96
7. 34.94
8. 3.508 or 3.5 pounds
9. 10,300
10. 819.20
11. 835.58

Problem Starters
Answers will vary.

Creating Problems
Answers will vary.

Show It on the Grid
Representations will vary. Following are some example solutions.

1. **1:4**
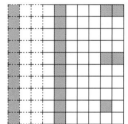
1:4 = 25%

2. **1:5**
1:5 = 20%

3. **3:4**
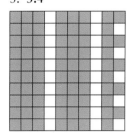
3:4 = 75%

4. **1:6**
1:6 = 16.6%

5. **5:8**
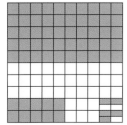
5:8 = 62.5%

6. **2:3**
2:3 = 66.6%

7. **1:3**

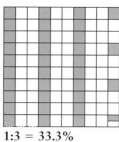
1:3 = 33.3%

8. **5:6**
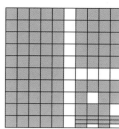
5:6 = 83.3%

9. **4:9**
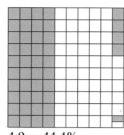
4:9 = 44.4%

Percent Templates
No answer.

Percent Card Sort

The following chart matches the percent with an equivalent expression.

Percent Given	Solution
A	7
B	3
C	2
D	6
E	9
F	8
G	4
H	5
I	1

Play It Forward

1. Shapes may vary. One possibility is

2. $15,000
3. $500
4. $20
5. 35 cheerleaders
6. 200 people
7. $48
8. 80 questions
9. 32 students
10. 750 tiles
11. $1,000
12. $37.50

Match It and Prove It

A. $6.75
B. $1.20
C. $16.05
D. $6.40
E. $75.60
F. $163.80
G. 15%
H. $156.75
I. $3.51
J. 20%
K. 19%
L. $39.90
M. $33\frac{1}{3}\%$
N. $5,670
O. $2.90

Increase Problems

1. 45% × $55 = $24.75 increase. $55 + 24.75 = $79.75.

2.

   $768 — 100% ... 120%

   100% = 5 cells, so 120% = 6 cells. To calculate the original cost, 768 ÷ 6 = 128. $768 − $128 = $640.
3. 100% = $38. It rose by $5.70. To calculate the percent of increase, 43.70 − 38 = $5.70. $5.70 ÷ 38 = 15%.
4. 6.8 billion − 2.6 billion = 4.2 billion growth. Divide 4.2 billion by 2.6 billion for an increase of 161.54%.
5. 9 billion − 6.8 billion = 2.2 billion growth. Divide 2.2 billion by 6.8 billion for an increase of 32.35%.

Percent Stories

1. 57; 25; 72; 44
2. 9.75; 74.75; 80; 7; 34
3. 21; 3.71; 71; 5; 43; 50; 10

Percent Math-O

Answers are included next to questions so that teachers can monitor the game.

What's the Problem?

Answers will vary.

Solving Problems

1. 96 baseballs and 80 softballs
2. 270 for grade six and 200 for grade seven
3. 58.33% of the ribbon
4. 1,020 child tickets